CRASH COURSE Drums

Hull College

ies

Printed and bound in the EU

Published by SMT, an imprint of Bobcat Books Limited
14-15 Berners Street, London W1T 3LJ, UK

www.musicsales.com

ISBN: 1-84492-014-3
SMT1100R

Drums

Pete Riley

smt

CONTENTS

ACKNOWLEDGEMENTS

THANKS TO...

- Joe and the kids, Billy and Ellie, for putting up with me being around even less while putting this project together.

- Jamie Humphries, Andy Staples and John Dutton for their wonderful playing and input on the backing tracks.

- Everyone at Premier, Zildjian and Vic Firth for providing such great equipment.

FOREWORD

INTRODUCTION

So now, having bought a drum kit, you need to make the transition from tapper to drummer, noisemaker to musician. But where to start? Without proper guidance it's easy to develop bad habits or spend time in the wilderness practising material you'll never use while other essentials remained untouched. One of the best ways of knowing what to practise is to listen and play along to music. It's a great way of understanding the role of the drums and why a drummer makes the different decisions within a tune – when to go to the ride cymbal, when to fill, etc. However, with that said, there can be no substitute for being shown the right material at the right time, and this is where *Crash Course: Drums* comes in.

A house is only as strong as its foundations, and *Crash Course: Drums* lays those foundations, starting with the grooves and fills you'll need to get you up and running and gradually adding each subsequent part at the right time. By the end of the book, with consistent work you'll be able to handle a variety of essential time feels and be able to hold your own in a band situation.

INTRODUCTION

So you want to learn to play the drums? Well, it's understandable. It always looks so much fun compared to other instruments; most non-musicians, if shown a room full of instruments, would probably gravitate towards the drum kit first. And there's something undeniably primal about hitting things with pieces of wood. From destroying Mum's new set of saucepans to tapping along to music on the steering wheel, it's something inside us – rhythm is part of our make-up. However, transferring this rhythmic appreciation to the drum kit is no mean feat. You no longer have just the hands to think about; the drum kit is the only percussion instrument requiring four-way co-ordination. Then there's learning some basic reading skills, playing in time, using dynamics and so on. But don't panic! Fortunately, the drum kit is probably the easiest instrument to get started on. In fact, within the first couple of days you should be able to play along to a tune on the radio. From there, of course, it does get more difficult, but by then it will be too late – you'll be hooked!

ABOUT THE BOOK

INTRODUCTION

This book is an eight-week drum course designed to take you from driving out the most basic beats to being able to play along with most tunes you might hear on the radio. Each week is broken down into daily lessons, and at the end of each week is a test, which comes in the form of a backing track requiring the use of some of the ideas and concepts learned throughout the previous week. Each week looks at different aspects of time playing along with fills, rudiments and co-ordination exercises. Each lesson is intended to take an hour or so to complete, although some will inevitably be more challenging than others, so don't get frustrated if you're unable to complete the lesson that day. Remember, Rome wasn't built in a day, or two months for that matter, so just take as long as it takes and enjoy your progress along the way. Here's a key to what you'll come across over the eight weeks:

 Timed Exercise – a rough guide to how long it should take to work through each exercise.

 Test Piece – an opportunity to test your ability in order to apply material learned over the previous week

 Quote For The Day – words of wisdom from renowned drummers

 CD Track – an opportunity to listen to some of the examples being played, shown with the corresponding track number

 Thought For The Day – nugget of information relating to the day's lesson

BEFORE WE GET STARTED

SETTING UP

Assembling a drum kit from scratch for the first time can be a daunting process – so many pieces of metal and so many height and angle possibilities. However, one important factor to consider right from the beginning is whether the kit needs to be left- or right-handed. I mention this because my first few days of drumming were a frustrating time as my right-handed friend had shown me where everything needed to be and hadn't taken my left-handedness into consideration. (Incidentally, all left-handed readers should simply reverse all of the stickings shown here. You'll soon get used to it!) Despite what some teachers say, I believe that a left-handed person should be encouraged to play this way, and most good teachers can accommodate it. One hybrid combination of this is when the feet are played right-handed and the hands play open-handed with the left hand leading. I've even had one student who played open-handed this way but then had his feet the other way around using a cable hi-hat and a double pedal attachment! These, however, are exceptions rather than the norm, and the point I'm making is that you should set up the kit in the way that feels most natural to you.

Once you've established which way around the kit will be set up, it's a good idea to get the main instruments – bass drum, snare drum and hi-hat – in place. Position the bass drum and hi-hat pedals so that they're situated in a comfortable position on either side of the snare stand and in line with the feet. Adjust the bass-drum legs to lift the front of the drum about an inch or so off the floor to create the ideal distance for the bass-drum beater to travel. The snare should be set just above leg height so that your hands don't hit your legs while you're playing the drum. Also, try to avoid

positioning the snare – or any other drums, for that matter – at an extreme angle. The wrist should as flat as possible when the stick makes contact. The hi-hats will need to be high enough above the snare to allow for reasonable movement, with the left hand sliding beneath the right as the hi-hat is played, but not so high that the right hand is chopping into the edge of the cymbals. Four to six inches should be fine.

The toms can then be added. Here, the floor tom – whether on legs or a stand – can be at a similar height and angle to the snare, positioned just to the other side of your right leg. The rack tom or toms should be placed so that movement off the snare and around the kit is smooth as possible.

Similar rules apply to cymbals, which should be placed where playing them is comfortable, as opposed to where they look good. If you have two cymbals – a ride and a crash, for example – try placing the ride over the second rack tom and the crash between the hi-hat and first rack tom. Again, avoid extreme heights and angles, as they will take their toll over long periods of playing.

One final important element of the set-up is the stool. First of all, avoid sitting too high or low. A good starting point is to keep your thighs perpendicular to the floor. Another consideration is how close you sit to the pedals – sitting right over the kit can create all sorts of balance issues and too far away puts things out of reach. Here, with the thighs in the position mentioned earlier, the lower legs should be pointing straight up to create a right angle or wider behind the knee.

ROLE PLAYING

Although the drum kit is generally viewed as a single entity, the various voices within the kit all have different roles that combine to create (hopefully) a unified sound. It's important to understand the roles of the different elements of the kit in order to complement the music in a way everyone will understand. This doesn't necessarily mean that you must copy everything that's been done before, but you should use it as a starting point. For example, if you tried playing time on the snare drum and using the bell of the ride cymbal for your backbeat, your listeners would be more likely to exchange glances than dance. With this in mind, here's a basic summary of the roles of the various elements of the kit.

SNARE DRUM

This is the point where it all started. Everything else Included in the modern kit is an addition to this drum. Originally used by marching drummers, band drummers began to play time on the snare before eventually moving to the cymbal a few years later. These days, we're used to the snare providing a backbeat that we can clap to – although, as the most articulate instrument on the kit, its also capable of creating a huge range of dynamics and nuances.

BASS DRUM

Originally played by a second person, with the advent of the bass-drum pedal early in the 20th century the bass drum was combined with the snare to allow one person to play the two parts. At first it was probably used for providing accents within the marching snare-drum parts, although later, in the swing era, it was used to lay down

Drums

quiet quarter notes while adding the occasional accent. By the time rock 'n' roll came along, the bass drum, like snare drum, had increased substantially in volume, and the two created a pendulum-type effect where, once you'd heard one, you expected the other. In contemporary music, these two are the loudest parts of the kit, with the bass drum spending most of its time locking in with the bass-guitar part.

HI-HATS

Originally called *sock cymbals*, hi-hats were first mounted on a pedal near the floor, an arrangement that made playing them with the hands impossible and only allowed the two cymbals to be splashed together. Eventually someone had the idea of mounting them on a stand, thus enabling them to be positioned next to the snare drum. At first they were used just for timekeeping with the foot, or occasionally as an alternative ride surface. These days they're the most commonly used riding surface in contemporary music.

RIDE CYMBAL

If you take a look at old pictures of drummers in the early 1900s, ride cymbals were really quite small by today's standards. Within a few years, though, fashions changed, and soon it wasn't uncommon to see a drummer playing a 24" ride cymbal! Nowadays a 20" ride is probably the most commonly used size.

The ride cymbal is still the main voice within jazz, but the hi-hats have superseded it in contemporary music. In fact, as volume levels have increased, some rock drummers no longer use a ride at all, choosing instead to play a large crash for a bigger ride sound.

Drums

In terms of when to use the ride versus the hats in most pop and rock situations, the ride cymbal is used to lift the dynamics (ie increase volume), so a simple rule of thumb would be to use the hi-hats during the verse and the ride cymbal during the chorus.

CRASHES, ETC

Usually found lurking at the end of a fill, the crash cymbal is like a full stop at the end of a sentence. Crashes can be played along with the bass drum, snare drum, toms or on their own to provide a variety of effects. Other cymbals – such as splashes, with their short, delicate sound, and china cymbals, with their dark roar – can also be used in this context to create alternative textures.

TOM-TOMS

In the early days of the 'traps' set, drummers were surrounded by a variety of percussion paraphernalia, from Chinese toms to woodblocks and cowbells. Most of these were used for effects, but one sound that caught on was the tom-tom, with its tribal sound. By the swing era, most kits carried two double-headed toms, and drum legend Gene Krupa had a generation of drummers emulating his 'Sing Sing Sing' tom-tom solo. During the '70s, the single-headed concert tom became popular, and at this time drummers could be seen (or perhaps not, in some cases) surrounded by every size of tom-tom possible. These days, double-headed toms in either four- or five-piece formats have retained their popularity.

Toms are generally used within fills, providing an alternative tonality to the snare. They can also be used to play the ride pattern, creating a dark, tribal sound.

MORE SETTING UP

In order for the different elements of the kit to work together, they must have the correct sound. For example, a snare tuned lower than the toms or a high-pitched bass drum might work in certain situations, but for most applications they would sound odd. When you buy a drum kit, you're really buying several different instruments, all of which need to be treated in different ways in order to create the sound most people associate with the drums. Here are some pointers for getting your drums sounding their best.

SNARE DRUM

As I mentioned earlier, the snare is the most articulate part of the kit, which is why it's positioned closest to you. In order to get the response necessary to get the sticks rebounding properly, the snare is tuned tighter and higher than the rest of the kit. Drum heads are also very strong, and so this drum will tune up really high and probably start sounding very choked and dry before any of the lugs or the shell give way (although don't hold me to this!). However, although it might feel easier to play double strokes, as well as giving an aggressive *crack* sound on the backbeat, with a drum tuned really high the sound will probably be very thin and unpleasantly sharp. A good rule of thumb is to tune tight enough that the drum creates a nice *crack* on the backbeat but not so high that you're unable to press the centre of the head inwards slightly.

The bottom head of the snare and the snare mechanism will also have profound effects on the sound and response of the drum. Again, the head needs to be fairly tight in order to get the snare to respond, but if it's too tight it can make the drum

sound brittle. Tightening the snare wires will also make the drum sound crisper, but if they're too tight they'll mute the drum *and* be stretched permanently, creating unwanted snare buzz. Try loosening the snare wires so that they're no longer in contact with the bottom head and then, while tapping the centre of the drum with a stick, begin to tighten them back up. As soon as you reach the point where they sound crisp, stop tightening.

As for the overtones created by the tight snare head, these can often get lost in a band rehearsal but can become annoying when practising or recording. Using one of the commercially available dampeners or even a small piece of tape placed towards the edge of the head should solve this problem.

BASS DRUM

At the opposite end of the frequency spectrum lies the bass drum. For most contemporary situations, this needs to be tuned as low as it will comfortably go. This means that there may even be wrinkles present, as long as they don't have an adverse affect on the sound. Along with a low tuning, the bass drum usually needs some form of dampening, too. This is necessary not only to stop unwanted high overtones but also to shorten the duration of the sound. The dampening – which could be in the form of a pillow, rolled-up towels taped to the head or similar commercially available devices – should really be in contact with both heads in order to reduce the overtones created by them both. It will also make the drum easier to play by reducing the movement in the batter head as the beater hits it.

Drums

TOM-TOMS

However many toms you're using, a good general rule of thumb is to try to cover as wide a tonal range as possible. So if, for example, you use three toms, tune the low tom as low as it will comfortably go and the high tom as high as sounds right when moving from the snare onto it. The second tom can then go somewhere in between the two. Tuning in this way makes it easier to hear movement between the different drums, which can easily blend together without special attention. When tuning the individual drums, try tuning the bottom head to the same pitch or slightly higher than the top to achieve the fullest sound.

Toms can sometimes need dampening when unwanted overtones are ringing for too long. This can be effected by using many of the commercially available products or, again, by using a small amount of tape. If you're trying tape, you may well find that it's the bottom head causing the problems, so be sure to try there first.

CYMBALS

In order to get the best possible sound and life out of your cymbals, make sure that when they're mounted on their respective stands they never come into contact with the metal of the stand. This requires cymbal 'sleeves' of some description to be in place on all stands. If you don't take care to do this, the metal-on-metal contact will cause the cymbal to wear away in the centre.

Also, avoid tightening down cymbals. This goes for hi-hats, too, which should be able to swing freely on their clutches. (Incidentally, the bottom hi-hat cymbal should always be

tilting slightly towards you by turning the spring-loaded screw found on the mount on which the bottom cymbal sits. Tilting the cymbal in this way prevents air from being trapped as the two cymbals come together, thus creating a louder *chick* sound.)

TECHNIQUE

In these early days, your drumming technique isn't going to be of the utmost importance, but bad habits are hard to break, so it's a good idea to start how you mean to go on. Here are some pointers for holding the sticks:

- Keep about 1" of the stick out of the base of the hand. This keeps the stick balanced within the hand.

- Avoid gripping the stick too tightly. This can cause blisters and, at worst, conditions such as tendonitis.

- Keep all of the fingers around the stick. So much control is gained from using all of the fingers – even the pinky!

- Lay the stick across the hand, with the butt against the heel of the hand, as opposed to under the wrist. This helps to keep the stick within reach of the fingers.

- Keep the first knuckle highest. In other words, the first joint of the first finger should be the highest point of the hand, as rolling the hand either way from this position creates an unnatural twist in the forearm.

Drums

When playing any part of the kit, try to avoid playing into its surface. Try to imagine that every part of the kit is red hot and the stick is your finger. Playing into the kit creates tension in the hands and is also great for 'pitting' and permanently damaging drumheads. Also, make sure the stroke is clear. Try avoiding flutters or unwanted double bounces, as these cause the stick to rebound.

With the bass drum, the chances are that you'll begin to play heel-down. Most drummers tend to do this until they develop the ability to play with their heels up and off the heel plate. Neither technique is right or wrong, although the heel-up technique offers more volume and power. However, with either technique – as with the hands – avoid playing into the drum; mashing the beater into the bass-drum head tends to deaden the sound of the drum and also retains tension within the leg between strokes. The hi-hats are slightly different in so much as, when they're played by the right hand, the chances are that the foot will be flat to the footplate. When they're stepped, however, playing heel-up will create a more cutting *chick* sound.

It's also worth considering *where* you hit the drums as well as *how*. For example, if you're playing a backbeat but not hitting the snare centrally, this will create a thinner sound as well as generate unwanted overtones. As a rule, try to hit all of the drums dead centre, while hitting crash cymbals with a sideways swipe, rather than straight into the centre of the cymbal, will help to pull the sound out of the cymbal and prolong its life, too. The ride, meanwhile, can be played in several ways – for example, the bow of the cymbal (ie the main body of the cymbal, excluding the bell) can be played with both the tip of the stick, for a thinner sound, or about a third of

the way down the stick, at the shoulder, for a thicker, crashier sound. In fact, although it's called the ride cymbal, don't be afraid to use it for the occasional crash; assuming it's not a really thick cymbal, you should find that it blends in reasonably well with your crash(es).

CLICK TRACKS

As drummers, our primary role is to keep time, and ever since the invention of the drum machine and the digital age, consciously or unconsciously, anyone listening to music has become aware of good timekeeping. As a result, it's now more important than ever for a drummer to be able to keep good time. The click track (which is basically a metronome) was first used on film score and jingle sessions, enabling producers to calculate the length of a piece in seconds and minutes. It was soon decided, however, that the feel and consistency offered by the click was preferable to the occasional tempo fluctuations inherent in the arguably more human performance of a click-free drummer.

Some drummers didn't handle this change particularly well and were replaced by a new breed of studio drummers who were able to lock in with drum machines, loops and programmed sequences.

Fortunately, good timekeeping isn't something that you're necessarily born with; it can also be developed. All that's needed is something to keep time with when practising, and to this end a cheap drum machine into which you can plug a set of headphones fits this bill perfectly.

Drums

READING

As confusing as it may seem, at times the ability to read music is a really useful tool.
For example, if you have 20 tunes to learn for a gig but not enough time in which to
learn them, you can write your own simple charts to get you through. These don't
need to consist of much – just the number of bars in each section, basic grooves, etc
– but I'm guessing that you haven't bought this book in order to learn how to read
music; your main aim is to learn how to play the drums. Unfortunately, in order to
show the different examples and exercises throughout the book, I've had to present
them all as musical notation. As a result, learning the various bits of theory
regarding note values and so on will be of great help in getting to the end. Don't
worry, though, if certain aspects of notation are confusing at first – after all, music
theory can be fairly complicated, rife with Italian expressions and strange symbols.
If in doubt, have a listen to the accompanying CD and hear how it relates to what's
on the page. Hopefully, the two will combine to make things easier.

Throughout the book I've chosen to use the American terminology for note values –
calling a crotchet a quarter note, for example. I did this for two reasons. Firstly, using
quarter and eighth notes etc is very logical; it's easy to see how the note values relate
to each other. Secondly, this terminology is used in most contemporary situations,
with crotchets and quavers being the preserve of the classical musician.

At the end of the day, the basics of reading music come down to learning to recognise
a few different symbols and some simple maths. It's not rocket science, and with a
little perseverance you'll soon have a very valuable addition to your musical abilities.

Here's the drum notation used throughout the book.

LEGEND

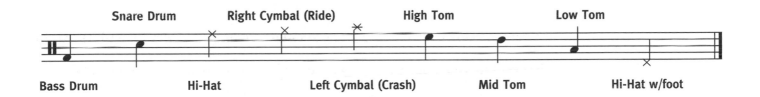

PRACTISING

In the same way as owning a Ferrari doesn't make you a racing driver, this book contains all of the necessary ingredients needed to make you a competent drummer, but the rest is down to you. Drumming is fun, and practising should be, too. Personally, I find practising one of the most enjoyable aspects of drumming, but for other people it's a chore. Regardless of which category you fall into, it's worth remembering that you get out what you put in. With that said, though, we all have days when we're tired or have things on our minds, making concentration difficult. Sometimes it's good to persevere, while at other times it's best to leave it. Either way, when practising, it's important to consider a couple of things.

Firstly, our brains absorb information best in small chunks. This means daily repetition is the best way of assimilating an idea. With this in mind, an hour a day will serve you much better than six hours one day a week.

Drums

Another consideration is how long your individual practice sessions last. Most people are able to concentrate fully for only about 20 minutes, so while non-stop four-hour practice session may seem like a good idea, you could probably achieve the same results in less time with more focused practice.

It's very easy to hit the practice room, stick on a CD and play away for a while only to discover that your hour is up and you've really worked on nothing. Knowing what it is you're going to practise will help maintain efficiency in your practice sessions. Also, try keeping a record of your progress; if there are few different areas that you're working on, keep a note of how long you spend on them and the tempos at which you work on them.

Making time available to practise can be difficult, especially as you get older and responsibilities increase, but by being organised and focused it's still possible to make progress in a relatively short space of time.

WEEK 1

DAY 1: QUARTER-NOTE TIME PLAYING

This first lesson looks at both reading and co-ordination. After first looking at the quarter-note pulse, this is then combined with a co-ordination exercise designed to help develop togetherness between the limbs as well as improve your reading skills and figure recognition.

THEORY

When we hear a drummer 'count off' a tune with the inevitable '1, 2, 3, 4', they're stating the *pulse* or *tempo* of the tune, which hopefully results in everyone starting at the same time and at the same speed. What's actually being counted is one bar of music that has been divided into four evenly spaced beats, which are quite logically called *quarter notes* (or *crotchets*, but more of that in a minute). So it stands to reason that, if we divided a measure into eight beats, we'd have *eighth notes*, or if we went the other way and divided the measure into two notes, we'd have *half notes*. Most contemporary music heard on the radio today has these four beats to the bar, although there are exceptions – a samba, for example, has a two feel, while a waltz has a three feel. Music of other cultures, such as Indian or Eastern European, has all sorts of odd pulses running through it, but in the West we tend to find comfort, through years of exposure to pop music, in the symmetry and simplicity of four beats to the bar – 4/4 (or common time), as it's known. This figure is called a *time signature* and is found at the beginning of any piece of Western music and at any point within it where the time signature changes. In a time signature, the top number

QUOTE FOR THE DAY

The quarter-note pulse is the most basic rhythmic element in contemporary music. – *Peter Erskine*

Drums

denotes the number of beats while the bottom tells us the value (a four tells us it's

quarter notes, an eight, eighth notes, etc). As musical notation, a quarter note is

represented by a note with a straight tail (Example 1a). If we want silence for the same

amount of time, we use a *quarter-note rest*. We can use different combinations of

these to place notes throughout the bar (Example 1b).

Example 1a   **Example 1b**

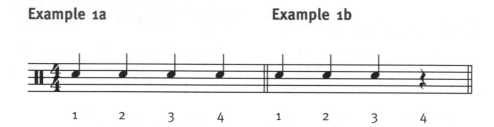

EXERCISE

Now, while playing all four quarter notes in the right hand on the hi-hat, try playing

through all of the different combinations shown in Example 2. When you've done

this, try the same thing but this time play the combinations with the left hand while

the right hand plays quarter notes on the hi-hat. This will develop reading skills as

well as co-ordination. Also, try counting the quarter notes out loud.

The next step is do the same thing, keeping the right hand playing the hi-hat but

this time reading the exercise with the left hand.

Drums

Example 2

Finally, we're going to try playing some time. To do this, the right hand will continue to play the quarter notes on the hi-hat and the left hand will join in on 2 and 4 only. This is our *backbeat*, so these two notes should be played at a reasonable volume. The bass drum will then play 1 and 3 (see Example 3). This is a time pattern on which most time-playing ideas are based. Once this is feeling comfortable, try working through the exercise, reading the figures on the bass drum. Remember, what the hands are playing shouldn't be affected by what the bass drum is playing. Getting all of the sounds to line up can be tricky, so stay with each bar until you're comfortable, and then move on to the next. Example 4 shows the first four bars played this way.

Example 3

Drums

 Example 4

THOUGHT FOR THE DAY

Counting is frowned upon in certain situations, but it does help connect the head with the hands, so to speak. Four measures of 4/4 can be counted like this: 1, 2, 3, 4 | 2, 2, 3, 4 | 3, 2, 3, 4 | 4, 2, 3, 4, so that the bars are also accounted for.

DAY 2: EIGHTH-NOTE TIME PLAYING

TODAY'S GOAL

Whilst the quarter note is the basis of most time playing, probably the most commonly used time pattern involves playing eighth notes in the right hand. In this lesson we're going to begin developing the ability to maintain this eighth-note time pattern whilst changing up the bass-drum pattern.

QUOTE FOR THE DAY

My whole take on learning, comprehending and dealing with means of expression, with what possibilities there are, boils down to trying to take this infinite thing called music and breaking it down into small amounts of easy-to-assimilate knowledge. – *Terry Bozzio*

THEORY

Eighth notes are counted as 1+2+3+4 (pronounced 'one-and-two-and', etc). An eighth note can be distinguished from a quarter note by a hook at the end of the stem (Example 1a). If, however, two eighth notes are placed next to each, they can be *beamed* together. This is done in a maximum of two groups of four, with the centre of the bar left clear for ease of reading (Example 1b). A silence for the duration of an eighth note – an *eighth-note rest* – is shown as a '7'-type shape (Example 1c).

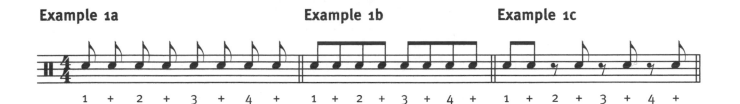

Example 1a   Example 1b   Example 1c

Drums

First, let's begin by playing eighth notes with the right hand on the hi-hat. Now, whilst maintaining this, we're going to try reading through Example 2 from Day 1, first on the bass drum, then on the snare. Example 2 here shows the first four measures played this way on the bass drum.

Example 2

Now let's play some time by adding a snare backbeat on counts 2 and 4. Adding the bass drum on 1 and 3 gives us a time pattern that is probably the most commonly used drum groove ever! Take some time to get this feeling really comfortable, making sure that the beats falling together on the quarter notes are *really* landing together.

Example 3

Drums

Now try working through Example 2 again on the bass drum. This will help you develop both time playing and independent playing. Watch out for points where two or more drum voices are played simultaneously, as it's at these points that it's easy to play a flam (two notes played slightly apart for a fuller sound) unintentionally. When playing time, we need these notes to fall exactly together. Example 4 shows the first four bars played this way.

 Example 4

THOUGHT FOR THE DAY

Listen for the togetherness of the notes and try to keep the right hand on the hi-hat as consistent and smooth as possible.

DAY 3: EIGHTH-NOTE BASS DRUM VARIATIONS

TODAY'S GOAL

Yesterday, I introduced the use of eighth notes on the hi-hat. Now we're going to begin incorporating them on the bass drum in order to create more interesting eighth-note grooves.

QUOTE FOR THE DAY

Every new idea I have and try to develop is a tiny piece in the big puzzle. I really take my time with everything I practise – months, years. – *Thomas Lang*

THEORY

So far we've looked at quarter notes and eighth notes and their respective rests. These two different note values can be used simultaneously in order to place notes at different places through the bar. In today's example, the bass drum is written on its own line below the stave, and although it's clear where the bass drum is falling in relation to the hands, notice how the different combinations of eighth and quarter notes are used to move the bass drum to different positions.

EXERCISE

The exercise shown in Example 1 is based around the same eighth-note hi-hat/2-and-4 snare-drum hand pattern, but this time the bass drum is slightly different. Work through it until you're comfortable with it.

Example 1

THOUGHT FOR THE DAY

Reading music, like regular reading, is all about figure recognition. Before you're able to reach this stage, though, it's really more about simple maths.

Drums

DAY 4: 16th-NOTE FILLS

TODAY'S GOAL

After spending some time sitting behind the kit, most drummers end up trying to play a fill down the toms consisting of four notes on each drum, from snare to floor tom. These groups of four are moving at twice the rate of our hi-hats, and are called *16th notes*. Today's lesson looks at a variety of ways of grouping these 16ths in order to create a one-bar fill.

QUOTE FOR THE DAY

Producer Kim Bullard took me aside and told me he had a specific rule about drum fills: 'Always flow out of the fill into the next section unless there's a specific musical reason not to'. – *Billy Ward*

THEORY

Whilst a single eighth note has a tail off its stem, a 16th note has two (Example 1a).

Like eighth notes, when two or more 16th notes are placed next to each other, they're beamed together in groups of four and on quarter notes (Example 1b). Sixteenth notes can be counted as '1-e-+-a, 2-e-+-a, 3-e-+-a, 4-e-+-a', etc (Example 1c).

Example 1a

Example 1b

becomes

Example 1c

1 e + a 2 e + a 3 e + a 4 e + a

EXERCISES

Each exercise shown in Example 2 is made up of a bar of 16th notes, and all are
played as hand-to-hand single strokes – R, L, R, L, etc. Example 2a begins by
playing all 16 notes on the snare, but from Example 2b onwards the hands move
around the drums. Practise each one slowly and be sure to maintain the hand-to-
hand sticking. These exercises should take five minutes each.

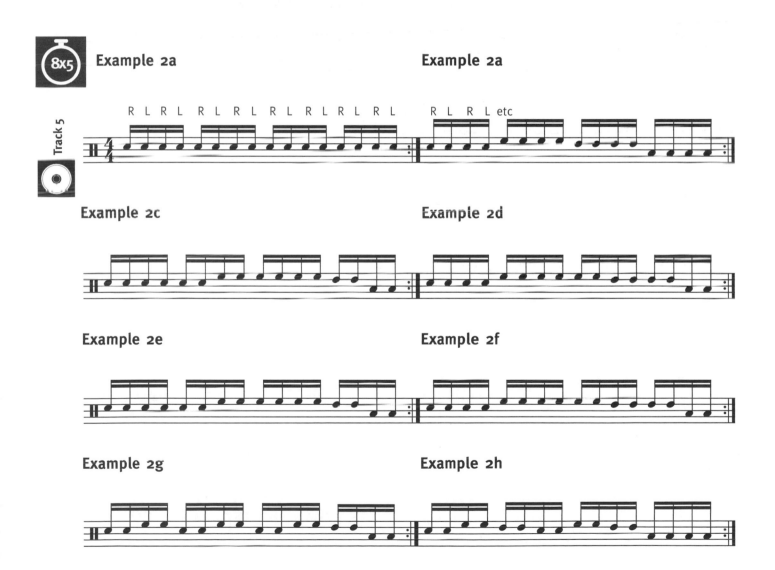

Drums

THOUGHT FOR THE DAY

When playing these examples, and fills in general, try to avoid the tendency to play the bass drum on all of the eighth notes. This is really the bass drum simply mimicking what the right hand is playing, and although in some situations it can be effective – after all, it was the signature sound of The Who's drummer, Keith Moon – it can often sound cluttered. Better still is to try keeping the left foot stepping either quarter notes or eighth notes on the hi-hat. This helps to maintain the time, giving both band members and audience a reference as you break away from playing time in order to play your fill.

DAY 5: OPEN HI-HAT PERMUTATIONS

TODAY'S GOAL

So far the left foot has had it easy, just sitting there on the hi-hat pedal, holding the cymbals together. However, now we're going to explore the idea of opening the hi-hats at various points in a groove in order to create subtle variations.

QUOTE FOR THE DAY

I just try to be part of the foundation. Everyone in the band can play; all you have to do is give them something strong to play over and it'll be fine. – *Steve Gadd*

EXERCISES

In drum notation, an open hi-hat is marked – usually above the stave – with an 'o', and the closed sign is a '+'. Simply put, this means that where you see an 'o' you allow the hi-hats to open and when you see a '+' you close the cymbals back to where they started.

The exercises shown in Example 1 look at opening the hi-hat for the duration of a quarter note. In each bar, the hi-hat closes on the next quarter note.

In Example 2, the hi-hat is open for an eighth note, so now the open-and-close motions with the left foot are on adjacent eighth notes. This is somewhat trickier to do, especially on the bars where the hi-hats are open on quarter notes, as the left foot has to close the cymbals on the more difficult upbeat.

Drums

Example 2

Track 6

Example 2

Track 6

THOUGHT FOR THE DAY

When opening the hi-hat in this manner, it's much easier to keep the left heel on the heelplate of the hi-hat at all times, as this offers stability while also allowing the leg to rest.

Drums

DAY 6: FILL IDEAS

TODAY'S GOAL

Today's lesson incorporates the use of the different subdivisions looked at so far and explores where they can be used.

THEORY

Songs are usually made up of several different sections: verse, bridge, chorus, etc. The transition between these different parts is often preceded by a drum fill. The purpose of the fill is almost to prepare the listener for the impending change. It also serves to create tension as the drummer breaks away from the main groove, with the release happening as the cymbal is crashed on beat 1 of the new section. What a drum fill *isn't* there for is to show off the drummer's prowess or the new lick learned the previous day. The right fill at the right time (and sometimes that can mean no fill at all!) can say so much.

QUOTE FOR THE DAY

The only thing I think about for a drum fill is that it be right for a particular part of the song. I hate having to play a fill for a fill's sake. – *Jim Keltner*

EXERCISES

The two bar patterns shown in Example 1 are each made up of one bar of time followed by another bar containing a fill. All of the fills shown here contain combinations of the different ideas and subdivisions covered so far. Work through them slowly, and then try to spend some time coming up with your own ideas.

Drums

10X5

Track 7

Example 1

THOUGHT FOR THE DAY

No matter how spectacular a fill, it must end at exactly the right place, so if you're aiming to hit a crash on beat 1 of the next bar, don't lose sight of the quarter note or your place in the bar as you play. This can bring disaster when playing with other musicians who, as you stumble over the barline, will suddenly feel as though they've lost beat 1, their most important point of reference.

Drums

DAY 7

Now we've reached the end of the first week, it's time for our first play-along test, this week's being in the form of an eighth-note pop/rock tune. The idea is that, by the end of today's lesson, you'll be able to navigate your way through the track, catching any accents, starting and stopping in the right places and playing the right groove.

THE TRACK

Today's track has a straightforward eighth-note pop feel and is made up of three different sections, which we'll call *verse*, *chorus* and *middle-eight*. The track begins with four bars of guitar, with the bass and drums entering on beat 4 of the fourth bar. The dynamic is marked *mf*, or *mezzo forte*, which means 'medium volume' – in other words, leave yourself room to increase or decrease the volume when necessary. The drums then play an eighth-note groove, with the bass drum playing 1 and the 'and' of 3, while the 'and' of 4 is also played every two bars. This groove is played for eight bars, after which a fill is played to take us to the chorus. This chorus is based around the same basic groove (although you could try opening the hi-hats slightly to lift the intensity a little) and is played for six bars, after which a fill takes us to the hits that end the chorus and middle-eight. This figure – which involves hitting the last eighth note in the bar – can be found on the penultimate bar of line 3, the first bar of line 4, the penultimate bar of line 5 and the first bar of the last line.

Once the first chorus is finished at the end of line 3, the two dots at the end of that measure are *repeat marks*, which send us back to the point where there are two identical dots facing the opposite way (in this case to verse 2 at the top of the page). The next time through, we play the chorus instead of the two measures that we played before the two marked '2x', or 'second time' – quite logically called the *second time bar* or, as American musicians would say, the *second ending*. This takes us into the fill that leads into the middle-eight. Note the hairpin-shaped sign below that bar which means *crescendo* (ie increase the volume).

The middle-eight then moves up from the hi-hat to the ride cymbal to complement the high point of the tune, and after six bars it ends with the same hits as those that appear at the end of each chorus. This time, however, the last note is held, with the drums restarting as they did at the beginning of the piece. From here we play one more verse and a chorus which ends with the same accent on the '+ 4', after which the guitar slows down (*ritards*), with the drums rejoining to play the last hit.

Try following the chart along without playing the CD, making sure that you're trying to read what's happening, as opposed to letting your ears pick up the tune. When you're ready, try playing the piece through. At this stage, don't worry too much about playing exactly what's played on the CD; instead, simply try to lock in with the track and keep your place within the tune.

OK, now here's the track:

Drums

Drums

THOUGHT FOR THE DAY

The part written out here is by no means the only thing that could be played along with the track, so once you're familiar with it, feel free to experiment with your own ideas. You could in fact use the track as a glorified metronome over which to practise any of the ideas you've been working on.

WEEK 2

DAY 8: 16th-NOTE HI-HAT PATTERNS

TODAY'S GOAL

Last week, we looked at 16th notes and the art of playing them as hand-to-hand fills down the toms. Today's lesson looks at how we can use this same idea to play time on the hi-hat.

QUOTE FOR THE DAY

The only time success comes before work is in the dictionary. – *David Garibaldi*

EXERCISES

Take a look at Example 1. Begin by playing 16th notes on the hi-hat, leading with the right hand. As you're doing this, count the 16th notes out loud. Now move your right hand from the hi-hat to the snare on beats 2 and 4. This is now the backbeat. Adding the bass drum on 1 and 3 provides the basic groove.

Example 1

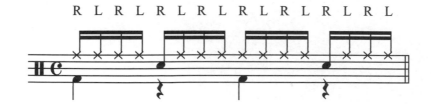

48

Example 2 shows some different bass-drum patterns, as well a few open-hi-hat variations. The first bar on the third line shows how, by playing both feet together on quarter notes, you can create a disco-type groove in which the hi-hat opens on the upbeat. This is followed by a couple of other open-hi-hat variations, as well as a final example which shows how the hands can be moved off the hi-hat and onto the kit to create 16th-note fills.

 Example 2

49

Drums

THOUGHT FOR THE DAY

In order for this groove to work, the 16th-note pattern needs to be played consistently and the backbeat on the snare needs to be played slightly harder than the hi-hats.

DAY 9: 16th-NOTE COMBINATION FILLS

TODAY'S GOAL

So far, when looking at 16th notes, we've played them in groups of four, but we can also combine them with eighth notes to create other useful figures.

THEORY

The two main figures used in this lesson combine one eighth note and two 16ths. These are combined in two different ways: firstly with an eighth note followed by two 16ths, and secondly with two 16th notes followed by an eighth note. These both sound very different, so it's important that you're able to differentiate between the two. Example 1a below shows the one-eighth/two-16th-notes figure, and this is then followed by the reversed two-16ths/one-eighth-note figure shown in Example 1b.

QUOTE FOR THE DAY

Living near New York City is very inspiring. I can go out and see a great drummer play every night. Then I come home recharged. – *Horacio 'El Negro' Hernandez*

Example 1a   **Example 1b**

Drums

In the exercises shown in Example 2, combinations of the figures mentioned today – as well as four 16th notes – are shown played down the kit from snare to floor tom. In each exercise, each beat moves to a different drum. As an extra challenge when working through the examples, try playing the left foot on quarter notes.

Example 2

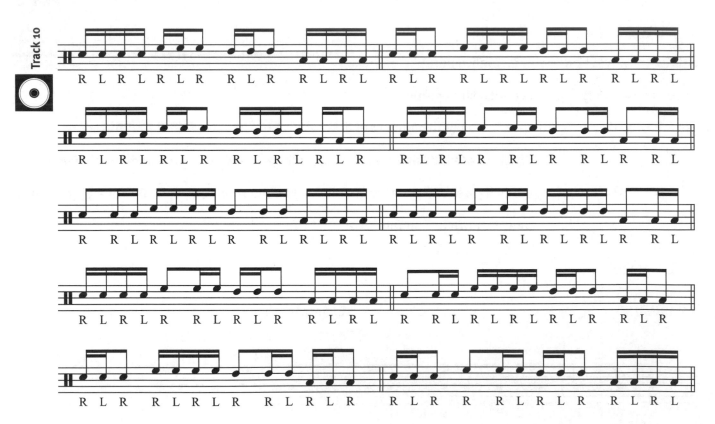

Once you're comfortable with each of the variations shown here, try playing three bars of time followed by one of the fills, as shown in Example 3. (Be sure to crash beat 1 of the following bar.) This will give you a four-bar cycle.

Example 3

R L R   R   R L R L R   R L R L

THOUGHT FOR THE DAY

Try to think of what the hands are playing as single strokes with the occasional note missing. In other words, the right hand always plays the eighth notes and the left plays upbeat 16ths. If you're keeping the sticking consistent, this makes it much easier to know where you are within a fill, as well making sure your right hand is ready to play a crash on the downbeat of the next measure (bar).

Drums

DAY 10: DOTTED EIGHTH-/16th-NOTE FIGURE

TODAY'S GOAL

Today's lesson looks at another commonly used 16th-note-based figure, this one involving playing the first and fourth 16th-note of each beat. As with previous figures, the aim here is to familiarise ourselves with how the figure sounds in order to be able to recognise it whenever it appears.

THEORY

The figure we're going to be looking at today is usually written as a *dotted* eighth note followed by a 16th note. (Placing a dot after any note increases its value by half. For example, dotting a quarter note – which is worth two eighth notes – adds half its value again, so it becomes worth three eighth notes.) Don't worry too much about dotting things at the moment, as things will make more sense as we carry on. In the meantime, Example 1 below shows this figure played on each beat in one bar.

Example 1

EXERCISES

In order to become familiar with the sound of this figure, Example 2 comprises several grooves that utilise it. Each exercise is based around a simple eighth-note hand pattern, so it's only the bass-drum pattern that changes. Placing the bass drum between hi-hat notes in this way can be tricky; to help develop a feel for it, you could try playing all of the upbeat 16th notes on the bass drum in order to create a continuous flow of 16th notes (Example 2a). You can then add the snare on beats 2 and 4 (Example 2b).

Example 2a   **Example 2b**

Next, the exercises in Example 3 all use different combinations of the dotted-eighth-/16th-note figure in various ways. The co-ordination required here can be quite demanding, so keep it really slow to begin with. Counting the 16th notes out aloud should help.

Drums

 Example 3

Track 11

THOUGHT FOR THE DAY

When placing the bass drum between the spaces in the eighth-note hi-hat

pattern, be sure to place them equidistant between the hi-hat notes. Again,

counting out loud can really help to line things up.

DAY 11: 'E'S AND 'A'S

TODAY'S GOAL

Two other figures that combine well with the dotted-eighth-/16th-note figure covered yesterday involve playing the 'e' and 'a'. Today's lesson looks at how the two can be combined to create some funky-sounding grooves.

THEORY

Example 1a shows a note played on the fourth 16th note – the 'a' – of a beat, preceded by a dotted eighth-note rest (yes, rests can be dotted in the same way as notes). Example 1b shows what this would look like if played on every beat along with our basic time pattern.

Example 1a　　　　　　　　　　**Example 1b**

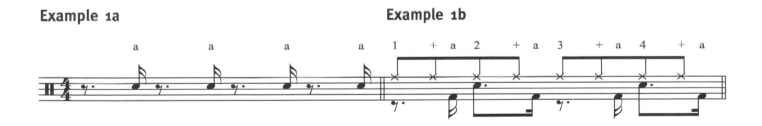

If we wanted to place a note on the second 16th – the 'e' of the beat – this could be notated as a 16th-note rest followed by a dotted eighth note. (A 16th-note rest can be distinguished from an eighth note rest by the fact that it has two lines at the top, rather than one.) Example 2a shows what this figure looks like if played on every beat, and Example 2b shows it played along with our time pattern.

Drums

Example 2a   Example 2b

Here are some more grooves that use different combinations of the figures used so

far. As before, try counting out loud, as this will really help to clarify where the notes

are falling.

8x10 Example 3

Drums

THOUGHT FOR THE DAY

By now, the differences between playing a note on the 'e', the 'and' or the 'a' of

the beat should be clear. In simple terms, the 'e' falls right after a downbeat,

the 'and' is the upbeat and the 'a' falls right before a downbeat.

DAY 12: PARADIDDLES

TODAY'S GOAL

When learning a melodic instrument, a lot of time is spent learning scales. The drum equivalent of this is probably *rudiments*, which are basically snare-drum patterns combining various stickings and accents. Traditionally, there are 26 rudiments to learn, although there are now many variations. In fact, years ago drum teachers would often insist that a student was able to play all of their rudiments before they had a kit, whereas these days people generally buy a kit and start tapping along to their favourite CDs straight away. Ideally there should probably be a middle ground, as some degree of facility between the hands can really help with general drum-kit playing.

QUOTE FOR THE DAY

I've always said that technique is innocent; it's the user who is responsible for the effect. As you develop maturity and experience as a musician, hopefully you learn to control the ego and make decisions that benefit the music. – *Virgil Donati*

In today's lesson we're going to begin our look at rudiments with the *paradiddle*, which is essentially a combination of single and double strokes that move from hand to hand.

Drums

EXERCISES

The basic sticking in Example 1 is R, L, R, R, L, R, L, L, but it becomes much more interesting if we add an accent on the first of each group of four whilst playing the remaining notes quietly.

Once you can play the basic figure (Example 1a), try moving the right-hand accent to the low tom and the left to the high tom, keeping all other notes on the snare (Example 1b). Next, try the same thing but playing the right-hand accent on the right cymbal with the bass drum and left-hand accent on the left-hand cymbal (Example 1c).

Track 13

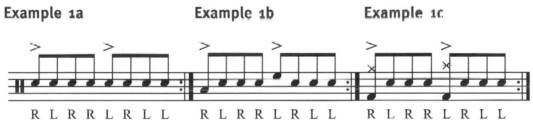

Example 1a	Example 1b	Example 1c
R L R R L R L L	R L R R L R L L	R L R R L R L L

It's also possible to play a longer version of the paraddiddle, the *double paradiddle*, by adding two more single strokes at the beginning of each group of four. Example 2 over the page shows the basic sticking, the accents on the toms and the accents on the cymbals.

Drums

 Example 2

Track 13

R L R L R R L R L R L L   R L R L R R L R L R L L   R L R L R R L R L R L L

Example 3 shows how the double paradiddle can also be played with two accents:

 Example 3

Track 13

R L R L R R L R L R L L   R L R L R R L R L R L L   R L R L R R L R L R L L

 THOUGHT FOR THE DAY

Once you're able to play the different variations, try picking up the speed, but not at the expense of accuracy or dynamics.

DAY 13: GROOVE AND FILL COMBINATIONS

TODAY'S GOAL

Today's lesson combines various elements looked at so far to create some interesting groove and fill ideas.

EXERCISE

Example 1 comprises some groove and fill ideas played as four-bar phrases consisting of three bars of time followed by a one-bar fill. Where necessary, feel free to

QUOTE FOR THE DAY

To love a drum fill without understanding why it works so well in that particular song is missing the lesson. – *Billy Ward*

work on both parts separately; you could also combine different grooves with different fills. This example is based around ideas we've already looked at, from bass-drum patterns and open-hi-hat effects to fills and paradiddles.

Example 1

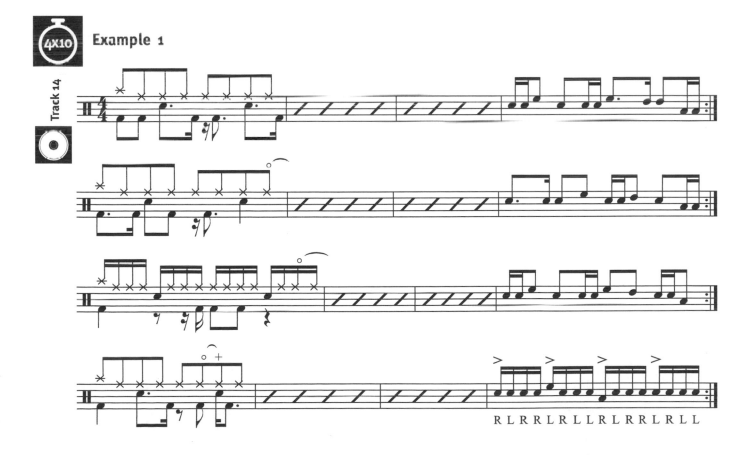

63

Drums

THOUGHT FOR THE DAY

The ideas presented here are by no means the only possibilities. Be sure to

spend some time exploring your own groove and fill ideas.

DAY 14

WEEK 2 TEST

This week's test looks at a chart based around a hand-to-hand 16th-note feel.
The track is a funk tune based around the same basic groove throughout.

THE TRACK

After the count-off, we're straight into an eight-bar vamp based around 16ths on the hi-hat, with the bass drum playing 2 and 4. This ends with the snare drum playing a simple figure along with the bass at the beginning of bar 8. A fill then takes us into the verse, which is a 16-bar sequence with a chord change on bars 9–12. At the end of this, a fill takes us to the *bridge*, which is an eight-bar sequence ending with an accent on the 'e' of 4. This is followed by a four-bar vamp which ends with the same figure that was used in the intro. After this, the same verse-bridge sequence repeats once more, and after the last bridge we return to the vamp for two measures. Then the whole band plays the verse motif as a *tutti* figure – in other words, everyone plays the same rhythmic figure together.

This tune is based around the same basic groove throughout, with the only difference being the move to the ride cymbal during the bridge, during which the bass player moves to a more Latin-style part, which the original bass-drum part will still work with.

As with the test at the end of Week 1, try to read along with the music first and make a connection between the information on the chart and the music itself.

CRASH COURSE
Drums

10 Week 2 test track

Track 15

16th-Note Funk
88bpm

66

Drums

If any part of the tune is proving too difficult, try playing through it with a simpler part. As you get more comfortable, work on the areas where the difficulty lies. For a new challenge, you could also try changing up the bass-drum pattern or try staying on the hi-hat during the bridge, perhaps opening the hi-hat on the upbeats.

WEEK 3

DAY 15: 12/8 GROOVES

TODAY'S GOAL

Up until now, all of the exercises we've looked at have been in 4/4. Today's lesson explores another commonly used time signature: 12/8.

THEORY

As you discovered on Day 1, a bar of 4/4 contains four quarter notes, with the first 4 indicating the number of beats and the second 4 informing us of their value – in this case, quarter notes. So 12/8 means that there are 12 beats, each with the value of an eighth note. These 12 eighth notes are divided into four groups of three, as shown in Example 1a:

> ### QUOTE FOR THE DAY
>
> I'm trying to bring more to the table. I like all kinds of music. And if you're gonna make yourself stick out, you have to investigate other kinds of music in order to bring something fresh to what you can do. – *Travis Barker*

Example 1a

EXERCISES

Playing the hi-hat on all eighth notes and placing the snare on 2 and 4 and the bass drum on 1 and 3 gives us a basic 12/8 groove, as shown in Example 1b. You may have heard this sort of groove on slow blues tunes.

Drums

Example 1b

The exercises in Example 2 show some variations on this basic pattern in which the

hands stay the same while the bass drum changes:

Example 2

Track 16

THOUGHT FOR THE DAY

This time feel can be a little strange to play at first, with the three-note spacing

feeling like there are either too many or too few notes, especially when dealing

with fills. You do, however, soon get used to it, and it can make a pleasant

change to the usual 4/4 feel.

DAY 16: SIMPLE 12/8 FILLS

TODAY'S GOAL

Now that you're able to play some different grooves in a 12/8 feel, it's time to look at some variations, including simple fills and open-hi-hat ideas.

EXERCISES

The exercises in Example 1 are all based around the same basic groove. The first four use open hi-hats for variations, the next two use simple tom fills and the final four use 16th notes to spice up beat 4.

QUOTE FOR THE DAY

Since playing is usually done in environments containing other people, I examine the flow of bars of playing before and after the new idea and ask, 'Have I completely ruined the feel that I established, or have I executed it smoothly enough not to bother anyone?' When I don't get dirty looks, I think I did OK. – *Mike Mangini*

Example 1

THOUGHT FOR THE DAY

Although these examples are written as repeating one-bar patterns, this is solely for practice purposes. Remember to use your fills and variations only when the music warrants it.

Drums

DAY 17: ONE-BAR 12/8 FILLS

TODAY'S GOAL

In yesterday's lesson, we looked at some one-beat fills to accompany a 12/8 feel. In today's lesson, we'll be taking some of these figures a step further by playing them over a whole bar.

EXERCISES

Example 1 comprises six one-bar 12/8 fills. Each uses a different combination of eighth and 16th notes, as well as different movements down the kit. Watch out for the orchestrations (ie which drums are being played) as well for the stickings.

QUOTE FOR THE DAY

Part of my thinking is that I want to be myself. I want to have my own voice. Achieving this is a long-term project. I'm always correcting my steering to stay on course. In the short term I ask, 'What do I need to do to become the best player I can be today?' The answer always reveals what I must work on to achieve this. – *David Garibaldi*

6x5 **Example 1**

Once you're able to play the examples individually, try playing each as a one-bar fill

after three bars of time, as shown in Example 2 below:

Example 2

THOUGHT FOR THE DAY

12/8 is a particularly difficult time feel in which to fill, especially at quicker

tempos. Try to locate some tracks at a variety of tempos to play along with.

DAY 18: DOUBLE-PARADIDDLE FILLS

TODAY'S GOAL

Several days ago, we began our look at rudiments with single and double paradiddles. Today's lesson looks again at the double paradiddle, as well as the closely related *paradiddle-diddle*, and applies them as fills in a 12/8 time feel.

QUOTE FOR THE DAY

Drummers are the train. We drive the truck. We focus on everybody. Our eye is on the big picture. – *Gary Novak*

EXERCISE

Examples 1a and 1b show the double paradiddle, with both single and double accents. As you know, this sticking requires the hands to switch each time it repeats. Example 1c, however, shows a variation of this sticking called the *paradiddle-diddle*, in which the sticking stays in the same hand as it repeats. Although not shown here, this can also be played leading with the left hand by reversing the sticking, and I recommended that you spend some time working on this.

Example 1a   **Example 1b**   **Example 1c**

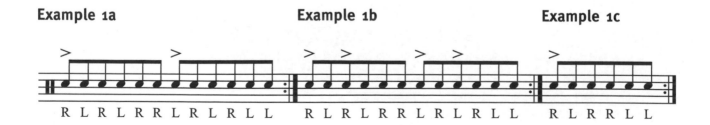

R L R L R R L R L R L L   R L R L R R L R L R L L   R L R R L L

Both of these stickings can be applied to a 12/8 feel as 16th-note-based fills. For example, if we play two repeats of the basic double paradiddle, it gives us a one-bar fill. The first three exercises in Example 2 show how this can be played on the snare, as well as moving the accents to the toms or the cymbals. The next three exercises show how it's possible to do the same with the two-accent variation. Finally, the last two exercises show how the paradiddle-diddle can be applied in this way.

When you can play each of these exercises, try playing each after three bars of time. Also, try coming up with your own ways of applying these different stickings.

Example 2

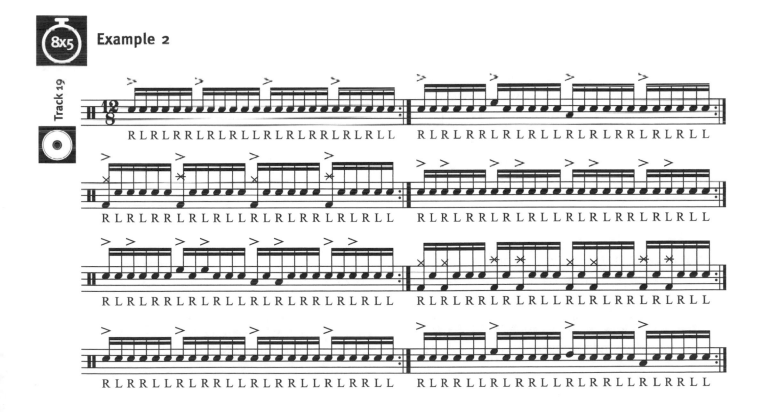

Drums

These stickings offer some great ways of moving around the kit in this time feel. Applying single paradiddles can also create some interesting phrasing ideas and are well worth experimenting with.

DAY 19: SINGLE STROKE ACCENTING

TODAY'S GOAL

Most aspects of drumming require single hand-to-hand strokes to be used, whether for a simple fill or for moving a flurry of accents around the kit in a solo. Today we'll take a look how to develop good single strokes, as well as how to place accents within them.

QUOTE FOR THE DAY

Over the years, I've tried to establish a personality on the drums that I hope can be recognised as my own style of playing. – *Terry Bozzio*

EXERCISES

The most important aspect of playing consistent hand-to-hand single strokes is in achieving an even sound with both hands, and as most people aren't ambidextrous, this usually requires some work. Begin by playing some slow eighth notes with the left hand, as shown in Example 1a. Try to get the stick to rebound off the drum, like bouncing a ball. Have a go with either hand, and then, once you're comfortable, bring both hands together so you're playing 16th notes, as in Example 1b. The next step is to work on building the tempo, although this shouldn't be at the expense of accuracy; be sure that you're still able to hear all the strokes evenly as the tempo increases.

Example 1a   **Example 1b**

Drums

The next step is to add some dynamics. Example 2 shows some different combinations of accented and unaccented notes, all of which are to be played hand-to-hand, and very slowly at first, with the focus being on playing the unaccented notes as quietly as possible, about an inch or so off the drum, and the accented notes at backbeat volume and in the dead centre of the drum.

Example 2

Once you're comfortable with these exercises, have a go at moving the accented notes to the toms or the cymbal and bass drum.

💡 **THOUGHT FOR THE DAY**

When practising single strokes, always try to feel the sticks rebounding off the surface of the drum, as playing into it destroys the energy within the rebounding stick and causes tension in the hands.

78

Drums

DAY 20: ACCENTING PHRASES

Yesterday we began to look at some single-stroke accenting exercises. Today's lesson focuses on joining together some of these figures to make more challenging accenting exercises.

QUOTE FOR THE DAY

Find the right weight sticks – too heavy can fatigue you and hurt your hands and wrists; too light will make you work too hard for the rebound. – *Dave Weckl*

Single strokes make up a big part of kit playing, and having the ability to place accents at any point within them will enable you to play seemingly complex figures with ease. Examples 1–3 over the page comprise a variety of eighth-note-based exercises aimed at developing your facility with single strokes. These should be played on the snare drum at first, but once you're comfortable with them it's important that you can play the accents elsewhere on the kit. Following these exercises is a list of just some of the possibilities at your disposal – try coming up with some of your own.

Drums

 Example 1

Track 21

R L R L R L R L etc...

 Example 2

Track 21

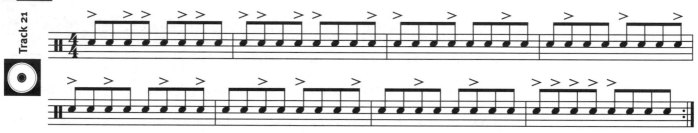

 Example 3

Track 21

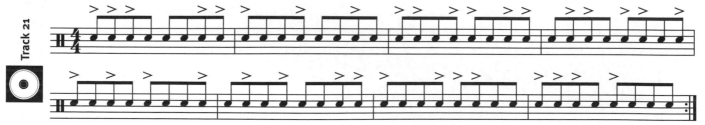

- Play right-hand accents on the floor tom, left-hand accents on the snare.

- Play right-hand accents on the snare, left-hand accents on the hi-tom.

- Play right-hand accents on the floor tom, left-hand accents on the hi-tom.

- Play right-hand accents on the right cymbal or bass drum, left-hand accents on the snare.

- Play right-hand accents on the snare, left-hand accents on the left cymbal and bass drum.

- Play right-hand accents on the right cymbal or bass drum, left-hand accents on the left cymbal and bass drum.

 THOUGHT FOR THE DAY

Maintaining a big difference in the dynamics is the key to getting these sorts of exercises to work. If the unaccented notes aren't played as quietly as possible, the accents simply won't leap out.

Drums

DAY 21

Today's play-along track is a 12/8 feel with a twist. Here the bass drum is playing the last eighth note of beat 2, creating a nice-sounding but rather tricky syncopation.

THE TRACK

Following the count-off, the track starts with a groove that sets the feel for the rest of the tune. It involves the bass drum playing beat 1 and the last eighth note of beat 2, while the 2 and 4 are played with a cross-stick. In order to create a thicker cross-stick sound, try turning the stick around so that the thick part of the stick hits the rim. Also, keep the tip of the stick about an inch or so from the edge of the drum, as too close to the edge or too far in will sound thin by comparison.

Following an eight-bar vamp and after a simple fill, the verse begins. This is an eight-bar section that repeats twice and then lifts into the chorus, where the cross-stick changes to an open snare and the right hand moves from the hi-hats to the ride. This section continues with the same bass-drum pattern, and after a fill at the end of bar 7, beat 1 of the next bar is held while a simple fill takes us back into the vamp. Again, this is played with a cross-stick on the snare for eight bars, after which the verse begins and an open snare is re-introduced. This same verse-chorus form then goes around for the guitar solo. We drop back down to the cross-stick for the last vamp, moving back to the open snare for the last verse and chorus, which ends with a *ritard* into the last chord.

Week 3 test track

Slow, bluesy feel

80bpm

Drums

WEEK 4

DAY 22: THE SWING FEEL

You may have heard the term 'playing with a swing feel'. This occurs when the middle note of a group of three notes is played as a rest, leaving only the first and last notes. Being able to play in a swing feel is an essential skill for any drummer, and today's lesson explores how it can be developed.

QUOTE FOR THE DAY

It don't mean a thing if it ain't got that swing. – *Count Basie*

SWING FEEL

When I first began to play drums, I recall that I was completely confused by my first encounter with a tune played in a swing feel. I could play a few different beats, but none of them seemed to fit over this new feel. Ironically, before 1950 the swing feel was the feel that every drummer would begin learning first, with the straight eighth feel only appearing towards the end of the '50s, with the advent of rock 'n' roll. Even then, there are recordings of the early jazz drummers struggling to come to terms with this new flattened-out feel and ending up playing somewhere between the two. These days the situation is reversed, with most young drummers starting off playing along to rock and pop music, the majority of which is played with a straight feel, making the switch to playing in a swing feel as difficult for them as it was for the early jazz drummers to play straight.

Drums

The swing feel is derived from *triplets* – groups of three evenly spaced notes fitted into a space normally allocated for two. Triplets can be applied to any of the subdivisions we've looked at – 16th notes, eighth notes, etc – and are shown as a '3' written above the notes in question. Eighth-note triplets can be counted as '1-trip-let, 2-trip-let, 3-trip-let, 4-trip-let', etc.

In Example 1, a bar of eighth notes is followed by a bar of eighth-note triplets played between the ride and snare. Notice how the snare moves from the '+' in the first measure to the 'let' of the triplet in the second. As you play this, you should feel the evenly spaced notes in the first bar begin to swing in the second bar. Example 2a and 2b, meanwhile, comprise a couple of simple exercises based around quarter notes in the right hand and an alternating snare-and-bass-drum figure.

The remaining exercises in Example 3 look at some simple swinging grooves. Here, the right hand plays quarter notes throughout while the bass drum and snare play variations.

Example 1

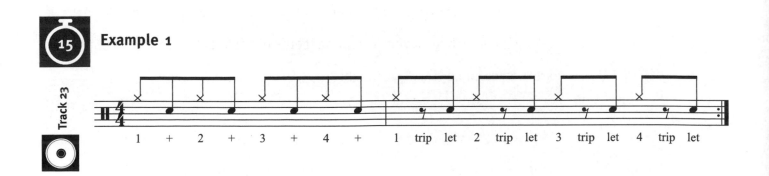

Drums

2X15 **Example 2a**   **Example 2b**

Track 23

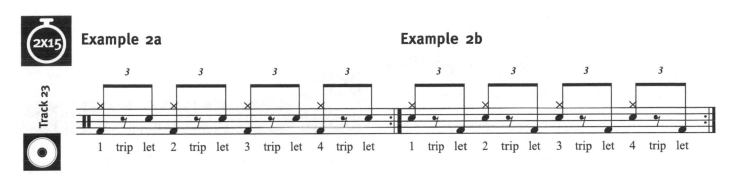

1 trip let   2 trip let   3 trip let   4 trip let   1 trip let   2 trip let   3 trip let   4 trip let

---

4X15 **Example 3**

Track 23

THOUGHT FOR THE DAY

The triplet feel is completely different to the straight feel associated with eighth

notes and 16ths. It feels more like the time is bouncing along than driving.

Drums

DAY 23: THE SHUFFLE FEEL

TODAY'S GOAL

The 12/8 feel explored last week can be played at fairly quick tempos – you only need to check out the legendary Jeff Porcaro's playing to appreciate that – but there comes a point as the tempo increases when, even with the necessary technique, the feel can become cluttered. By losing the middle note of each group of three, a new, more swinging feel called the *shuffle* is created.

QUOTE FOR THE DAY

You can gain a lot of the original concepts from formal training, but then you must have practical experience, which means getting out and spending some time playing in bands.

– Harvey Mason

THEORY

Examples 1a and 1b below show a basic 12/8 feel, both with and without the middle note from each group of three. With these middle notes removed, this pattern gives us our shuffle, a feel derived from the jazz/swing feel and often used in blues. A shuffle is usually written in 4/4 as opposed 12/8, and in order to show the three-note groupings on each beat the eighth notes are written as eighth-note triplets, as shown in Examples 2a and 2b.

Example 1a   **Example 1b**

Example 2a   **Example 2b**

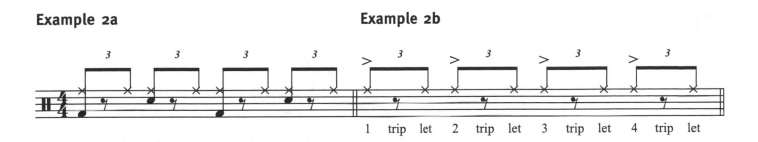

In order to give the shuffle its correct feel, we need to apply some dynamics to the right-hand pattern. To do this, we need to play the quarter notes using the shoulder of the stick on the edge of the hi-hats and the 'let', or third partial, of the triplet using the tip of the stick on the top of the hi-hats, as shown in Example 2b. Once you're feeling comfortable with this, you can add the bass drum on quarter notes and the snare on beats 2 and 4 to give a basic shuffle groove.

From here, you can go one of two ways, usually dictated by what the bass player is playing. If the bass player is playing a walking bass line consisting of quarter notes, this four-on-the-floor bass-drum pattern will work well. (We can also change what the left hand is doing to make the pattern drive even more, but more of that later.) If, however, the bass player is playing a rhythm similar to that played by your right hand, it can be better to change to the bass drum, just as we did with eighth- and 16th-note feels. Over the page are some variations to try.

Drums

9X10   Example 3

   Track 24

DAY 24: THE TEXAS SHUFFLE

TODAY'S GOAL

Today's lesson covers that essential drum groove, the Texas shuffle.

EXERCISES

Bandleaders often judge a drummer on his or her ability to play a good shuffle feel. This usually comes down to the drummer's ability to play with some snap, swing and consistency. Often when drummers are asked to play a shuffle, they're expected to play what's known as a *Texas shuffle*, which involves playing quarter notes on the bass drum while both hands play a shuffle feel but with slightly different accents. The right hand plays the same pattern as the one looked at in yesterday's lesson, while the left, although playing a shuffle feel, accents only 2 and 4.

While this sounds easy, it does require some independence of movement. To develop this, you could try playing with both feet on quarter notes, then play a few bars of the right hand on the ride cymbal (Example 1a), then a few bars of the left on the snare (Example 1b) and finally try combining the two (Example 1c).

Drums

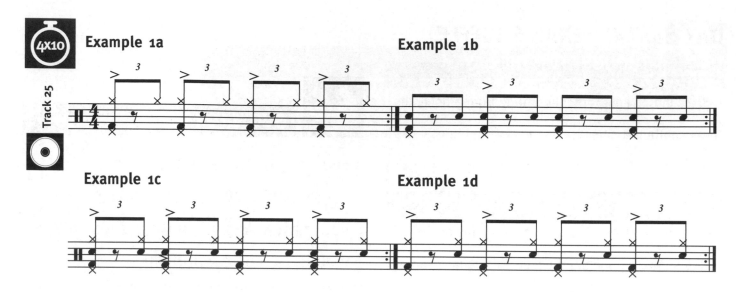

Example 1a   **Example 1b**

Track 25

Example 1c   **Example 1d**

Example 1d shows another useful shuffle-independence exercise. It involves playing a shuffle in the right hand and only the third partial of the triplet – the *skip note*, as it's known – in the left. This appears easy enough, but if you're to maintain the accents in the right hand, it can be quite tricky. Example 2 shows another couple of shuffle variations where certain notes are excluded from the left hand:

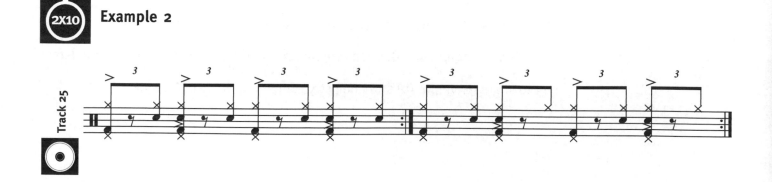

2X10 **Example 2**

Track 25

Drums

THOUGHT FOR THE DAY

When playing shuffles, the thing that really makes them work is consistency. If you hear a drummer playing a shuffle, the chances are there won't be fills every few bars; instead a steady, unrelenting groove is laid down.

Drums

THOUGHT FOR THE DAY

The three-over-two pulse is probably the most commonly used of all polyrhythms. It's also traceable back to Africa, and is thought to be the origin of the jazz ride-cymbal pattern.

DAY 26: EIGHTH-NOTE TRIPLET FILLS

TODAY'S GOAL

Now that we've explored a variety of shuffle-related time feels, it's time to develop some fills with which to complement them.

EXERCISES

We'll begin by playing a one-bar phrase made up of hand-to-hand eighth-note-triplets on the snare. Once you're comfortable with the first exercise in Example 1, work through the rest individually.

QUOTE FOR THE DAY

Usually I'm concentrating on the quarter notes. That's where my focus has to be, to keep the tempo locked. Whatever subdivisions I play in those spaces, I make sure they're locked in with the quarter note so that I don't rush them.

– Steve Gadd

Example 1

Also try playing each as a one-bar fill following three bars of time. In order to do this smoothly, it's necessary to break away from the shuffle feel and play a pick-up note in the left hand on the last eighth-note triplet of the preceding bar. This pick-up note can be played a couple of different ways, either with the left hand or the bass drum. Example 2 shows these played after one bar of time:

Example 2

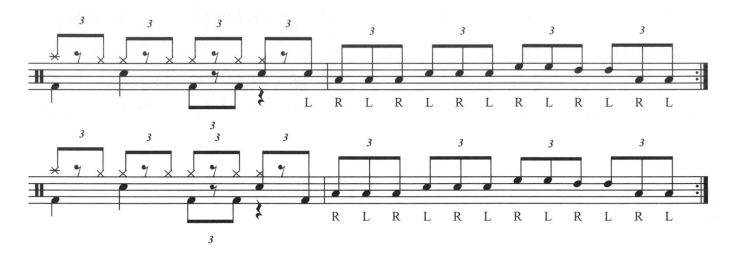

THOUGHT FOR THE DAY

The appeal of your shuffle playing isn't going to rely on your being able to play great fills, but this will be a bonus. Just remember that feel is where it's at – the rest is just the icing on the cake.

Drums

DAY 27: EIGHTH-NOTE TRIPLET ACCENTING

TODAY'S GOAL

It's also possible to add dynamics to our eighth-note-triplet ideas in the same way as we did with our eighth-note exercises. Today's lesson looks at some basic exercises to develop this, as well some different ways of orchestrating them around the kit.

QUOTE FOR THE DAY

In some ways my father restricted me a lot, technically. He would tell me that what I was playing was way too busy. What he was doing then is exactly what a lot of producers do now in the studio. – *Simon Phillips*

EXERCISES

Let's begin by playing a bar of eighth-note triplets as single strokes but playing the quarter-note beats as accents and all remaining notes as quietly as possible (Example 1a). Then try the same thing, but this time accenting the skip note (Example 1b). This will give you the ability to play accents on the downbeat and the upbeat.

Once you're able to play these individually, try playing them as two-bar phrases.

Example 1a   **Example 1b**

Drums

Next up are some more downbeat/upbeat combinations. Once you're able to play the examples on the snare drum, try moving the accents around the kit in the ways discussed earlier. Be sure to keep the unaccented notes on the snare, as shown in Example 2.

Example 2

Example 3, meanwhile, includes four examples of fill orchestrations derived from Example 2.

Example 3

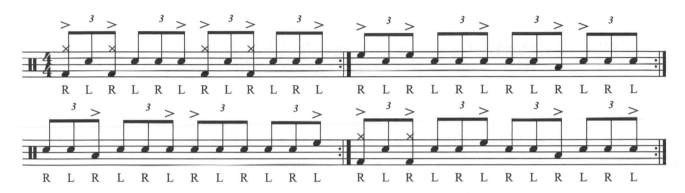

R L R L R L R L R L R L R L R L   R L R L R L R L R L R L R L R L

R L R L R L R L R L R L R L R L   R L R L R L R L R L R L R L R L

THOUGHT FOR THE DAY

Try combining these fill ideas with some time playing, perhaps one bar of

time followed by a one-bar fill, or three bars of time and a one-bar fill. Also,

be sure to try to come up with your own fill ideas using different accents and

co-ordination ideas.

Drums

DAY 28

WEEK 4 TEST

This week's test track is a blues shuffle that moves between two different shuffle

feels. As an extra challenge, there's a solo section based around some rhythmic hits.

THE TRACK

Today's track starts with an eight-bar vamp which stops on beat 1 of bar 8, where the

keyboard introduces the melody and the 12-bar blues form begins. This form then

repeats, the second time building to a walking Texas shuffle feel for the guitar solo.

After the guitar solo comes the drum break. This is again over a 12-bar form, which

builds into one final chorus and ends with a traditional blues ending.

THOUGHT FOR THE DAY

The form for this track is straightforward, as are the two different grooves.

Probably the most demanding part has to be the drum breaks. You could, of

course, choose to play time through them, although it's much more fun to try

to fill in between them. Try to keep an ear on the click, and think triplets!

 Week 4 test track

Track 29

Blues shuffle

105bpm

Drums solo through hits

103

WEEK 5

DAY 29: DOUBLE STROKES

TODAY'S GOAL

Today's lesson looks at developing the *double-stroke roll*. This involves playing two even notes in each hand, with the end result hopefully sounding as smooth as single strokes.

QUOTE FOR THE DAY

Find a good teacher to study with. More knowledge is always very motivating.

– *Dave Weckl*

EXERCISES

What, you might ask, is the point in developing double strokes only for them to sound like singles? Well, in certain situations, double strokes have a number of advantages over singles. Firstly, they allow orchestrations around the kit that would be impossible with singles. Secondly, they can be placed between accents, allowing a hand-to-hand sticking to be maintained. And thirdly, they can be played quicker, allowing you much greater control over dynamics than with single strokes.

When people first begin to play double strokes, there's a common and understandable tendency to throw each stick down and allow it to bounce, creating a second stroke. Unfortunately, the laws of physics dictate that, without some extra force, the second note is never going to be as loud as the first. Here we'll look at how we can develop even-sounding double strokes as well as explore some possible uses.

When practising double strokes, the first thing to do is make sure the notes are evenly spaced. A commonly used phonetic is 'mummy, daddy', and if we continue looping them around, this is the same consistent quality we want from the hands (Example 1a). Next up we need to make sure all of the notes are played at the same volume. When we break this down, we discover that, in fact, they're actually not! In order to achieve an even feel, the second note needs to be accented, so it's not so much 'mummy, daddy' as 'mum**my**, dad**dy**' (Example 1b). It may seem odd to emphasise the second note in this way, but as the tempo picks up you should hear the two notes begin to blend together.

Example 1a   **Example 1b**

The next step, once you're able to play consistent-sounding doubles, is to try to move between single strokes and double strokes. The first exercise in Example 2 shows a bar of single-stroke eighth notes followed by a bar of double-stroke 16th notes. The key when working on this and all the remaining exercises is to try to get all notes, whether single or double, to sound the same. The remaining exercises in Example 2 are all one-bar permutations of this first exercise.

It's also possible to do the same thing with eighth-note triplets. Example 3 shows some different combinations of single and double strokes that move between eighth-note and 16th-note triplets.

Drums

7X5

Example 2

R L R L R L R L   R R L L R R L L R R L L R R L L

R L R L R R L L R R L L   R L R R L L R R L L R L

R L R R L L R L R R L L   R R L L R L R R L L R L

R L L R L L R L L R L L   R R L R R L R R L R R L

Example 3

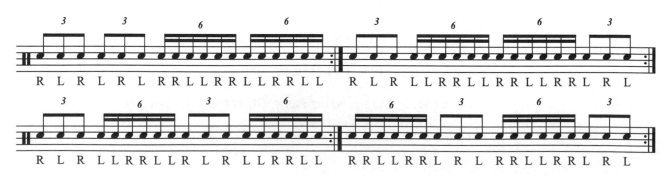

R L R L R L R R L L R R L L R R L L   R L R L L R R L L R R L L R R L R L

R L R L L R R L L R L R L L R R L L   R R L L R R L R L R R L L R R L R L

THOUGHT FOR THE DAY

By working through these exercises at a variety of speeds, you should begin

to develop your ability to play and use double strokes. However, make sure

that, as the tempo increases, the articulation remains accurate – without the

necessary control, the doubles can begin to move in the netherworld

between double strokes and buzz strokes if the stick is allowed to bounce

more than twice.

107

DAY 30: ACCENTS WITHIN DOUBLES STROKES – BASIC FIGURES

TODAY'S GOAL

Earlier in the book we looked at placing accents within groups of four single strokes, moving the accent one note later in each subsequent exercise. In today's lesson we're going to be replacing the unaccented notes in those exercises with double strokes to create seven-, six-, five- and three-stroke rolls, along with a few variations.

QUOTE FOR THE DAY

I warm naturally to any drummer whose ideas and approach are strong, even if he doesn't quite have the ability to carry them out. – *Bill Bruford*

EXERCISES

Example 1 shows the same four basic accent permutations we covered back when we looked at single strokes. In each of the exercises that follow, all of the unaccented notes are replaced by two 16th notes played as a double stroke. This first example creates the rudiment known as a *seven-stroke roll*, with the remaining three examples simply being variants of that. When working on this and all of the remaining exercises, try to keep the double strokes down in volume in relation to the accents, which should leap out if the correct difference in dynamics is created.

 Example 1

108

Example 2 does exactly the same thing, only this time using two accents. In the first two exercises, the accents are played on downbeats and upbeats respectively, while the remaining exercises are the same as the first four exercises, only with two accents. These examples are all *six-stroke rolls*.

 Example 2

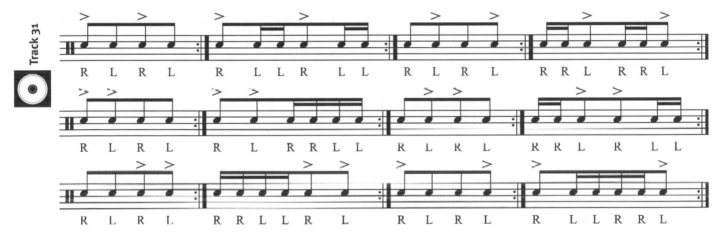

 THOUGHT FOR THE DAY

Once you're able to play these variations, the next step would be to start moving the accents off the snare and around the kit. When doing this, all of the double strokes should remain on the snare. This is where keeping the doubles down in volume really comes in to play, as without the difference in dynamics, the accents don't have the desired impact.

DAY 31: ACCENTS WITHIN DOUBLES STROKES – COMBINATIONS

TODAY'S GOAL

In the previous two lessons, we looked at developing double strokes and how they can be combined with different accents. In today's lesson, we'll be looking at how a similar approach can be taken with triplets, as well as how figures can be combined to create longer phrases.

QUOTE FOR THE DAY

Technique is an endless path to allow me to make the music I want to make. It's also a dangerous thing for drummers to practise for many hours but not listen to records.

– Horacio 'El Negro' Hernandez

EXERCISES

Let's begin with a look at applying double strokes to the two triplet figures looked at last week. Example 1 shows how we can replace the unaccented notes in both single-stroke examples to create what are known as *hand-to-hand five-stroke rolls*.

Example 1

Next up we can combine all of the double-stroke figures looked at so far to create longer phrases. Example 2 shows a variety of combinations. Each is shown first as accents within single strokes, then with all unaccented strokes doubled.

 **Example 2**

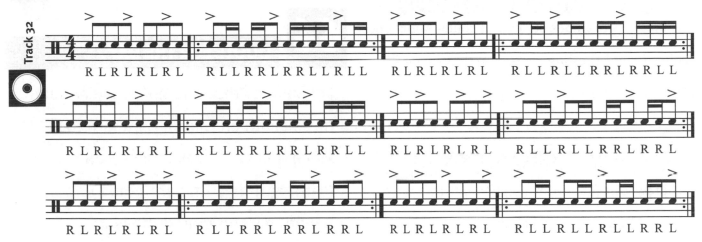

As soon as you're comfortable, begin moving the accents around the kit. Example 3

shows the right-hand/left-hand tom and cymbal orchestrations covered earlier.

Example 3

THOUGHT FOR THE DAY

Be sure to explore your own ideas – for example, you could keep the right hand

on the hi-hat, the left on the snare and add a bass-drum hit to all right-hand

accents. Wherever you choose to play the accents, the important thing – as

before – is that the unaccented notes are played much quieter than the accents.

Drums

DAY 32: ACCENTS WITHIN DOUBLES STROKES – ONE-BAR COMBINATIONS

TODAY'S GOAL

Today's lesson concludes our look at double strokes by exploring longer phrasing ideas as well as eighth-note-triplet-based phrases.

EXERCISES

Example 1 shows four two-bar eighth-note accent patterns followed by the same thing with the unaccented notes played as double strokes. Be sure to maintain the correct difference between the subdivisions, as well as the difference in dynamics.

Next, Example 2 shows three eighth-note-triplet phrases followed by their double-stroke equivalents. Here, the eighth-note-triplet phrases are similar to those covered on Day 27, and indeed the same kind of process can be applied to those patterns.

Probably the easiest way to develop these exercises is to move between the single-stroke and double-stroke versions, playing each through perhaps four times. This will enable you to ensure that the phrasing is correct as you move into double strokes.

Drums

Example 1

Track 33

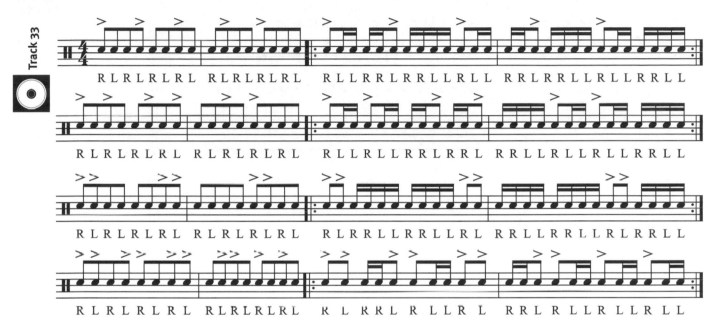

RLRLRLRL RLRLRLRL   RLLRRLRRLLRLL   RRLRRLLRLLRRLL

RLRLRLRL RLRLRLRL   RLLRLLRRLRRL   RRLLRLLRLLRRLL

RLRLRLRL RLRLRLRL   RLRRLLRRLLRL   RRLLRRLLRLRRLL

RLRLRLRL RLRLRLRL   R L RRL R LLR L   RRL R LLR LLRLL

Example 2

Track 33

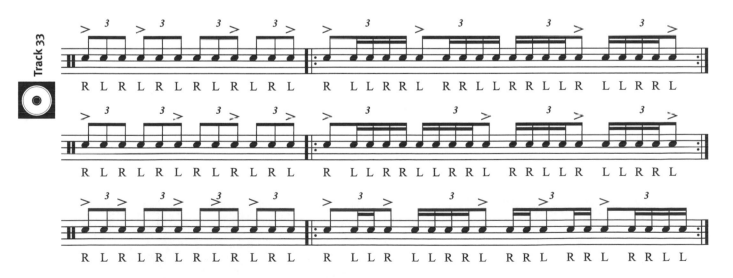

RLRLRLRLRLRL   R LLRRL RRLLRRLLR LLRRL

RLRLRLRLRLRL   R LLRRLLRRL RRLLR LLRRL

RLRLRLRLRLRL   R LLR LLRRL RRL RRL RRLL

Drums

THOUGHT FOR THE DAY

Being able to place accents within double strokes this way opens up many possibilities around the kit, so once you're able to play the exercises shown here, begin to move the accents to different parts of the kit in order to come up with your own double-stroke ideas.

DAY 33: HI-HAT VARIATIONS

TODAY'S GOAL

Sometimes when playing time it can be nice to add some different inflections on the hi-hat to keep things interesting. These can range from simply opening the hats on the last eighth note to more demanding things, such as the use of double strokes. Today's lesson explores some hi-hat variations that can be added to spice up an otherwise straightforward groove.

QUOTE FOR THE DAY

It's not about playing all your chops; you want to make the music work. In the past I've been guilty of playing something just because I can, but now I try to play for the music.

– Zach Danziger

EXERCISES

The first four exercises in Example 1 involve incorporating single-stroke 16th notes to add some extra movement to a basic groove.

 Example 1

Drums

We can also use our newly developed double-stroke skills to play 32nd notes on the hi-hat, as shown in Example 2. To do this, try playing the doubles on the top of the hi-hat (much easier to avoid stick rebound this way) and all other notes on the edge.

 Example 2

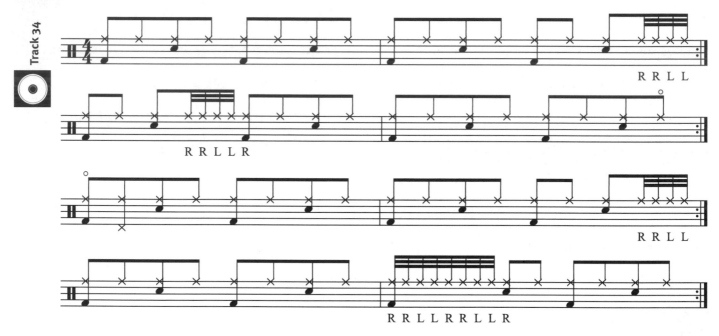

R R L L

R R L L R

R R L L

R R L L R R L L R

 THOUGHT FOR THE DAY

These kinds of ideas are great for adding some life to an otherwise uninteresting pattern, but beware: playing them every couple of measures can detract from the groove, so once you're able to play them, choose your moments carefully.

DAY 34: UPBEAT EIGHTH-NOTE IDEAS

TODAY'S GOAL

One of the most commonly used figures in eighth-note-based music is that where, instead of hitting beat 1, the last note of the previous bar is hit. As drummers, we need to develop the ability to set up this figure without interrupting the flow of time.

EXERCISES

Example 1 shows a variety of ways in which the 'and' of 4 in the first measure can be set-up. The first exercise shows how the figure can be hit by lifting off the hi-hat on beat 4, giving time to prepare to hit the 'and' of 4. You should then be able to get back down to the hi-hat to resume time on beat 1. The remaining exercises are all variations on this basic move.

> ## QUOTE FOR THE DAY
>
> There are different qualities required from a musician. Is it jazz, rock, Latin, metal, reggae, folk, classical, or something else? Each of these styles has different technical and musical requirements. Technique is not about faster and louder; it's about control and making playing easier. – *Thomas Lang*

Example 1

(continues...)

Example 1 continued

 THOUGHT FOR THE DAY

The play-along track in the next lesson is an ideal place to begin applying these different ideas, once you're ready. And these are by no means the only possibilities – much bigger fills could be played by starting earlier – although it's the simplest ideas that will maintain the time flow better.

Drums

DAY 35

WEEK 5 TEST

This week's test piece is a straight eighth-note rock/metal tune with an up-tempo, driving feel and lots of emphasis on the 'and' of beat 4. So let your hair down and turn that stereo up to 11!

THE TRACK

Today's tune starts out with a figure that combines the concepts looked at over the last couple of days: double stops and hitting the 'and' of beat 4. After this figure, we're straight into a churning, eight-bar guitar riff that is repeated twice. The second time through, we go into the B section and up to the ride cymbal. The eight-bar section here ends with cymbal chokes on all of the upbeat eighth notes (apart from the last one in the last bar, which takes us into the next section). A cymbal choke is created by hitting the cymbal with the right hand while the other hand – holding the stick with the last two fingers, leaving the first two fingers and thumb free – grabs the cymbal almost as soon as it's struck. This creates a short, sharp stab effect that's used a lot in rock and metal.

Following the B section, sections A and B are repeated again when we reach the C section. Watch out for the first note here because, unlike most of the tune, it's actually on beat 1. Here the drums fill around the picked guitar part that goes around four times, after which the drums enter with a half-time feel. After eight bars, the

drums double time back to 2 and 4, and after six bars a double-stop-type build-up
between the floor tom and snare ending on the 'and' of 4 lifts us out into the last B
section. At the end of this section, instead of hitting all four upbeat eighth notes, we
only hit the first three. The guitar then fills in the next bar, leaving us to hit the 'and'
of beat 4.

 Week 5 test track

Track 36

Driving eighth-note rock/metal

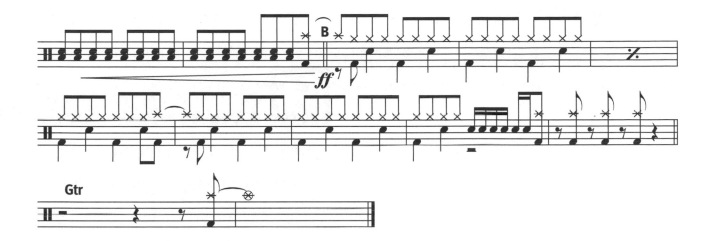

Gtr

THOUGHT FOR THE DAY

Once you're able to play through this tune, try to come up with your own ideas.

For example, try changing up the bass-drum patterns, or try some different

fills, especially at the beginning of the C section.

WEEK 6

DAY 36: GHOST NOTES

Whilst playing a simple groove, it's possible to create extra movement within it via the use of *ghost notes*. Today's lesson explores what these are and how and where they can be used.

QUOTE FOR THE DAY

Even though I've always admired players with well-developed technical skills, my favourite type of player is one who knows how to play songs.

– *David Garibaldi*

EXERCISES

If you take our eighth-note time pattern in the right hand, you can use your left hand to fill in some of the upbeat 16th-note spaces. In order for this to work, these left-hand notes must be played very quietly in relation to the backbeat. Example 1 shows how these ghost notes can be added to the same basic groove.

Example 1

Things get really interesting when we begin to add some 16th notes on the bass drum. Example 2 shows a couple of variations on this. Meanwhile, another great-sounding ghost-note groove is based around our hand-to-hand 16th-note hi-hat

Drums

pattern. Here, however, the left hand, instead of staying on the hi-hat, plays the same

part but as ghost notes on the snare, while the right hand still moves from the hi-hat

to the snare on 2 and 4, as before. Example 3 shows two versions of this groove, the

first with the bass drum on 1 and 3 and the second with a more syncopated pattern.

 Example 2

 Example 3

R L R L R L R L R L R L R L R L   R L R L R L R L R L R L R L R L

 THOUGHT FOR THE DAY

Ghost notes can really spice up your playing by creating another sound and movement. However, they will only work if there is a significant difference in volume between the ghost notes and backbeat. When working on this, try to keep the left hand as loose and relaxed as possible. Playing the ghosted notes slightly off centre can also help to emphasise the difference in volume.

CRASH COURSE
Drums

DAY 37: ALTERNATIVE SNARE PLACEMENTS

When drummer Harvey Mason came up with the drum groove on Herbie Hancock's Headhunters' tune 'Chameleon', it changed people's perceptions of where a drummer could play a backbeat and still sound funky. On the track, instead of playing the snare on 2 and 4, Harvey plays beat 4 as normal but the first snare one 16th note early, on the 'a' of beat 1. This funky new approach changed the future of drumming by allowing drummers to play in a more syncopated way whilst still grooving. In today's lesson, we'll look at some of the different possible snare-drum placements and how they can be used to create funky-sounding grooves.

QUOTE FOR THE DAY

I gain amazing pleasure from fitting into the situation, regardless of what it is. Rather than going to that place where you're getting off, you back off a little bit so that the entire group is getting off. – *Harvey Mason*

EXERCISES

Example 1 shows nine different grooves that use variations on the basic 2-and-4 backbeat. In some patterns, the 2 and 4 remain and other accents are added, whilst in others certain snares are moved to somewhere completely new. Often, these new snare placements are simply places where a bass drum would normally be played along with a regular 2-and-4 backbeat, creating a funky, syncopated feel.

In grooves like these, it's essential that the hi-hat remains constant, as this is your reference for the time, so it's a question of developing the co-ordination between the hands to enable the left to play a backbeat anywhere without affecting the right.

Drums

Example 1

THOUGHT FOR THE DAY

These kinds of grooves make a fun change to the regular 2-and-4 backbeat and are especially effective if played without variation, enabling the listener to pick up on the syncopation. You could also try incorporating the ghost-note ideas as well to create some dynamic and funky grooves.

DAY 38: QUARTER-NOTE AND UPBEAT EIGHTH HI-HAT GROOVES

TODAY'S GOAL

Right at the beginning of the book, we started off looking at playing some simple time patterns along with a quarter-note pattern on the hi-hat to develop some basic independence. However, just because we left it behind, this doesn't mean that the quarter-note pattern in the right hand becomes redundant once you're able to play eighth notes. It is, in fact, used a lot in rock and funk situations. So, today we're going to look at playing a variety of grooves along with it, as well as moving it to the upbeat eighth note for a completely different feel.

QUOTE FOR THE DAY

It's important to understand what's going on around you, as far as what the bass player is doing, what the lyrics are saying and what the guitar player is playing. Listening is all-important.

– Josh Freese

EXERCISES

The first exercise in Example 1 shows the starting point: quarter notes all round. The next three are more demanding as the quarter note in the right hand remains while more syncopated bass-drum patterns are introduced. Try to keep your hands constant as the bass drum changes here. This kind of feel is often used in funk situations, but if played with more open, trashier hi-hats, it applies equally to rock and metal.

Example 1

Track 39

Next up is a feel that can really play havoc with the co-ordination, as the hi-hat is now almost playing in the cracks between the backbeats. Here the hi-hat has moved one eighth note later, to play all of the upbeat eighth notes. In Example 2, I've tried to ease you in gently by starting off with some eighth-note bass-drum exercises.

 Example 2

 Track 39

 THOUGHT FOR THE DAY

When playing eighth notes in the right hand, it's easy to feel where the other notes fall in relation to them, whereas the quarter-note-based time patterns shown here are especially tricky due to the space between notes in the right hand. However, with a little perseverance these quarter-note patterns should start to feel comfortable and add some new possibilities to your time playing.

Drums

DAY 39: ACCENTED HI-HAT PATTERNS

TODAY'S GOAL

Today's lesson expands the quarter-note patterns looked at yesterday. So far when playing eighth-note time on the hi-hat, our focus has been on playing evenly accented eighth notes. In today's lesson, we're going to look at how the quarter-note and upbeat eighth-note accents can be applied to eighth notes to create a subtle change in feel.

QUOTE FOR THE DAY

I had to invent my own notation – absolute hieroglyphics, really, but I understood it. The charts looked like the old *Batman* show: Play 16 bars, *POW!* Boom-Boom, dun-de-DUN-dun – that kind of thing. Let me say this to drummers out there: Learn to read!

– Phil Collins

EXERCISES

Let's begin by playing eighth notes on the hi-hat – simple enough. Now try accenting all of the quarter notes. To do this, try playing the accented notes on the edges of the cymbals using the shoulder of the stick whilst playing all of the unaccented upbeat eighths on the tops of the cymbals using the tip of the stick. Accenting the hi-hat in this way can be useful when playing a feel that requires only quarter notes on the hi-hat, as the unaccented notes, if played quietly enough, will blend into the background, while the constant eighth-note motion is much easier to play than lone quarter notes, which can tend to feel wooden. Example 1 shows a few different grooves to try along with this hi-hat pattern.

Example 1

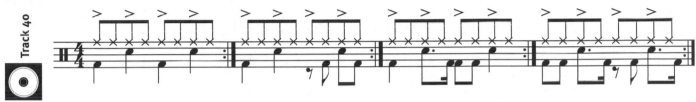

Another, even more useful hi-hat accenting idea is to accent all upbeat eighth notes. This creates a nice 'lift' to the feel, but is also more difficult than our previous downbeat accent, which tends to have a more instinctive feel. Work through the exercises in Example 2 slowly, making sure that, as the bass drum changes, the hi-hat remains constant.

Example 2

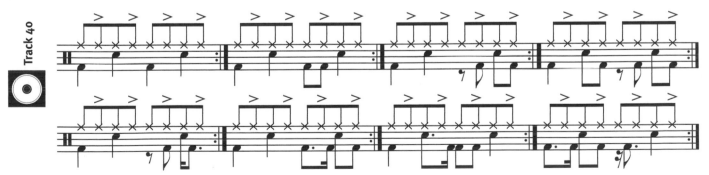

Drums

These two-accent patterns can have a profound effect on the feel of a tune. For example, if the upbeat variation is added at the right time, it can really lift a tune, creating an almost double-time effect. Quarter-note accents within the eighth notes can also work well as an alternative to just quarter notes by maintaining the eighth-note framework. However, beware of situations that require driving eighth notes, where accenting the quarter note can make the time feel sluggish, giving the impression that momentum is falling away on the quieter upbeat eighth notes.

Drums

DAY 40: EIGHTH-/16th-NOTE HI-HAT PATTERNS

TODAY'S GOAL

We're going to continue this week's time-playing theme in today's lesson, where we're going to look at some alternative hi-hat patterns that involve the use of 16th notes.

QUOTE FOR THE DAY

So many people try to make you feel it's wrong or not cool to listen to this or that kind of music. It's so selfish for anyone to do that to you. – *John Otto*

EXERCISES

If we take a basic eighth-note hi-hat pattern but add an extra note on the last 16th note of each beat, we get the pattern shown in bar 1 of Example 1, which can make a nice alternative to straight eighths. This initial bar is followed by some alternative bass drum patterns to try.

 Example 1

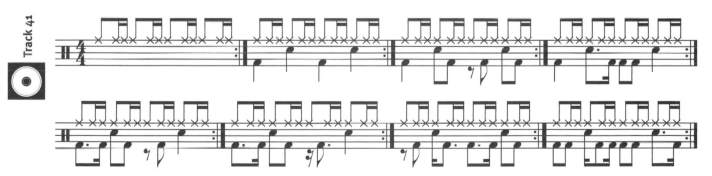

We can also try a similar approach, but this time adding the second 16th note of each beat. The first bar of Example 2 shows what this would look like, and this is followed by a familiar selection of bass-drum variations.

Drums

 Example 2

 Track 41

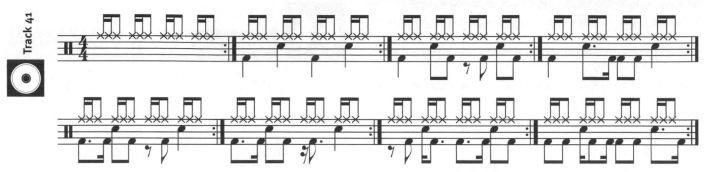

THOUGHT FOR THE DAY

These right-hand patterns can make an interesting alternative to eighth and

16th notes and can also work well when played on the ride cymbal or floor tom.

DAY 41: BASS DRUM EXERCISES

TODAY'S GOAL

Developing the ability to control the bass-drum pedal can be a difficult and frustratingly slow process. Today's lesson looks at building control, stamina and accuracy via a variety of exercises.

EXERCISES

The first exercises here address both bass-drum control and co-ordination. In Example 1a, the hi-hat plays quarter notes while the bass drum moves from eighth notes to eighth-note triplets to quarter notes, playing one bar of each. Be sure to start this exercise at a speed at which you're able to play 16th notes on the bass drum, or thing will just fall part as you move up through the subdivisions. Example 1b shows how this pattern can also be played the other way around, this time with the bass drum playing quarter notes while the hi-hat changes.

QUOTE FOR THE DAY

I used to argue with Buddy Rich about warming up. Buddy would say that he never warmed up. I would say, 'Yes you do.' He would say, 'What are you talking about, Bellson?' I would say, 'What about when you rehearse with the band before each performance? That's warming up!' He would eventually agree.

– Louis Bellson

5 **Example 1a**

Track 42

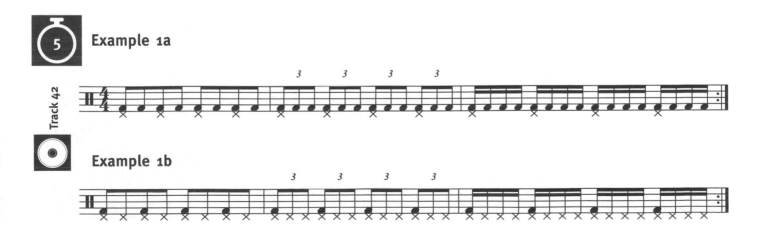

Example 1b

Drums

The exercises in Example 2 are based around some simple bass-drum figures played along with a basic time pattern with the hands. Here, the bass-drum pattern is shown on its own in the first bar, followed by the bass-drum and time patterns combined. These exercises are all focusing on developing the ability to play two adjacent notes on the bass drum, and they should really help you develop some control and stamina. Start slowly, picking up speed only when everything is feeling comfortable.

 Example 2

THOUGHT FOR THE DAY

As every athlete knows, developing strength and endurance takes time – after all, you don't get up one morning and run a marathon. Exercises like these are no different; it'll take time to get them up to any kind of speed, so don't be put off if progress seems slow. Keep returning back to them regularly and you'll soon see some results.

DAY 42

WEEK 6 TEST

The four-on-the-floor disco feel – based around the bass drum playing all four beats in the bar and the hi-hat playing 16th notes – is just as prevalent today as it was in the '70s. Today's test track is based around this disco/dance-type feel and moves between a four-on-the-floor bass feel and a simple funk groove.

THE TRACK

Today's tune begins with four bars of keyboards, after which the guitar enters, along with the hi-hat, playing 16th notes. After four bars, the main groove begins, where the same 16th-note pattern on the hi-hat continues, along with all four quarter notes on the bass drum and 2 and 4 on the snare. At bar 8, the band drops out for beats 1 and 2, although on the CD I played a cymbal on its own, with the band picking up on beats 3 and 4.

From here, we're into the A section and the groove changes to more of a funk feel. On the CD, the groove is based around eighth notes, apart from an extra snare added on the fourth 16th note of beat 2. This section is an eight-bar cycle that repeats, but the second time around there are some quarter-note-to-eighth-note accents that run through bars 7 and 8.

Drums

From here we have eight bars of the B section again for eight bars, then back to the

A for eight, and finally back to B. At the end of this B section we move into the C

section at which point you could move the right hand over to the ride cymbal for a

change of feel. This section then leads into a breakdown section consisting of keys

and drums and lasts for eight bars. The ninth bar is our fill back into the B section,

which repeats twice, ending on beat 1 following the eighth-note accents.

Week 6 test track

continues...

Drums

Week 6 test track continued

THOUGHT FOR THE DAY

As with the previous test tracks, the drum part here is by no means set in stone; it's simply a guide to help get you playing through the track. With this in mind, be sure to try out your own groove ideas. For example, in the breakdown section, instead of playing time you could even try playing a drum solo for eight bars!

WEEK 7

DAY 43: HAND/FOOT COMBINATIONS

TODAY'S GOAL

Whilst a lot of mileage can be found in moving around the kit playing single strokes, some really interesting ideas appear when the bass drum gets involved. Today we'll be looking at incorporating the bass drum with the hands to create some great-sounding fill ideas.

QUOTE FOR THE DAY

Some things would take a year or two before I could play them. I would play them at soundchecks or when I was working on my kit until I got to the point where it felt right. When the time to play it in front of an audience comes, I really have to focus. – *Terry Bozzio*

EXERCISES

The first exercise in Example 1 shows some different combinations that can be played between the hands and bass drum. These exercises form the basis of the rest of today's examples, so I recommended that you spend some time familiarising yourself with them. Once you're able to play them on the snare, try moving your hands around the kit while keeping the dynamics as even as possible between the hands and bass drum.

Example 1

Now it starts to get interesting as these ideas are combined to create one-bar phrases. Example 2 shows just a few of the many possibilities to be found. Again, these patterns really come to life once you start to move your hands around the kit. The final exercise shows one possible orchestration idea.

Drums

8x10   **Example 2**

Track 44

THOUGHT FOR THE DAY

Combinations such as these make for some really interesting fill and/or solo

ideas, but where things really start to get interesting is where groups of two

are incorporated on the bass drum...

Drums

DAY 44: COMBINATIONS USING TWO BASS-DRUM STROKES

Today's lesson expands on the fill ideas looked at yesterday, only this time we'll be incorporating figures that use groups of two on the bass drum to create some impressive-sounding fill and solo ideas.

EXERCISES

Example 1 shows the two figures that form the basis of all of the following examples. They both consist of four-note groupings, the first starting with the hands, the second with the bass drum. Once you're able to play these basic figures, try moving your hands down the drums, as shown in the first pattern from Example 2. Any of these patterns could be used as a one-bar fill, but the only problem with the first one is that, in order to hit beat 1 of the following bar with a cymbal and bass drum, you need to play three consecutive notes on the bass drum – difficult for any drummer to do at tempo. It's possible, however, to come up with some really interesting fill ideas by combining our two original figures. Check out the remaining patterns in Example 2. Try spending some time picking up the speed as well as exploring your own ideas.

QUOTE FOR THE DAY

Unlike when practising, when performing in public, I'm not going to play anything I can't do. This evaluation works for me and always puts me in the right state of mind to enjoy my playing.

– *Thomas Lang*

Example 1

R L   R L

Example 2

Track 45

THOUGHT FOR THE DAY

In these exercises, the bass drum has its work cut out, making them great for

developing your bass-drum speed and stamina.

Drums

DAY 45: EIGHTH-NOTE TRIPLET COMBINATIONS

The hand-and-foot combinations looked at in the previous lessons can also be applied to triplets. Today's lesson looks at some different combinations of these, along with some orchestration ideas.

EXERCISES

The first triplet figure that most people probably discover first is the right/left/foot combination. Examples 1–4 are based around this idea, starting out on the snare and then moving down the toms, then keeping the left hand on the first tom while the right hand moves between the snare and floor tom, and finally keeping the left hand on the high tom while the right hand moves down the kit.

QUOTE FOR THE DAY

Goals, both short and long term, need to be achievable by reaching, but must be kept within reach. Otherwise it's only going to lead to disappointment. One brick at a time, slowly but steadily.

– *Bill Bruford*

This combination can also be played with the bass drum first – ie foot, right hand, left hand. Example 5 shows the basic figures while Example 6 shows how it can be played down the toms. Example 7 shows another possibility that involves playing quarter-note triplets in the right hand whilst filling in the spaces on the bass drum. This could also be played with the right hand or even with a hand-to-hand sticking.

Examples 8 and 9 are based around our original combination, here in a right-foot-left format, while Example 10 features a six-note group – four with the hands and two with the feet. Try moving the hands around the kit or splitting them between drums.

Drums

10X10

Track 46

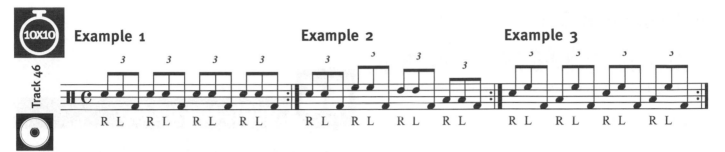

Example 1

RL RL RL RL

Example 2

RL RL RL RL

Example 3

RL RL RL RL

Example 4

RL RL RL RL

Example 5

RL RL RL RL

Example 6

RL RL RL RL

Example 7

R R R R R R

Example 8

R L R L R L R L

Example 9

R L R L R L R L

Example 10

R L R L   R L R L

THOUGHT FOR THE DAY

With a bit of work, these figures can all be played at pretty impressive speeds and can make great fill and solo ideas. To begin incorporating them into your playing, try playing some time first and then the above exercises as fills. Don't be afraid to start slowly, focusing solely on maintaining the rolling-triplet feel.

Drums

DAY 46: FLAMS

One important rudiment yet to be explored is the *flam*, which is essentially when one hand falls slightly before the other to create a thicker sound. The stickings involved can also mean that within single strokes it becomes possible to play two different sounds simultaneously, but more of that later. First, let's look at the basic moves.

QUOTE FOR THE DAY

The music tells you what to play, when to play and when not to play.

– *Horacio 'El Negro' Hernandez*

EXERCISES

I'm sure that at some point we've all played a flam of some description, possibly whilst hitting the floor tom and snare simultaneously at the beginning of tune. In this instance, the chances are that a right-hand flam is being played, in so much as it's the right hand that falls last, as in Example 1a over the page. Obviously, the second way is to play a left-hand flam, with the left hand falling last (Example 1b). The third approach is to play the flams moving from hand to hand (Example 1c), which is actually quite tricky, especially at speed.

The key to playing any of these examples lies in the dynamics. You'll notice that in each example the second note is accented, so when attempting these you should try to keep the first note much quieter than the second.

Drums

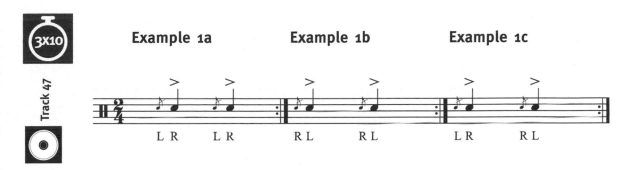

Next up we're going to place another unaccented note between the flams. This can

be done leading with the left or right hand (Examples 2a and 2b) or, as in Example

2c, moving from hand to hand. This is a rudiment called the *flam tap*.

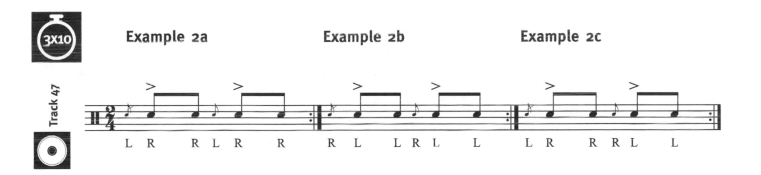

The next example explores playing a flam every three notes. This can be done in

either of two ways: if we want to play it with a hand-to-hand motion, we can use the

flam accent (Example 3a); or if we want to keep it in the same hand, we can use

what's known as a *Swiss Army triplet* (Example 3b).

Drums

Example 3a   **Example 3b**

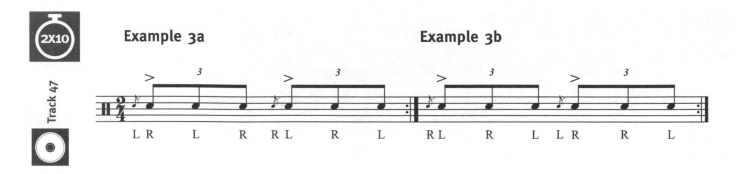

Finally, if we want to play a flam every four notes, we can do it within single strokes,

as shown in Example 4a, or moving from hand to hand, as in Example 4b. Notice the

sticking used in a 4b; if it looks familiar, it's because it's based around a paradiddle,

which is why this rudiment is called a *flam-paradiddle* or *flam-a-diddle*.

Example 4a   **Example 4b**

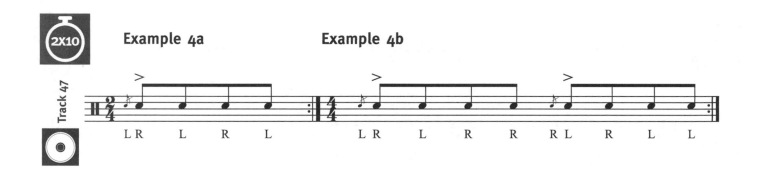

 THOUGHT FOR THE DAY

These moves can seem difficult at first, but when moved to the kit they offer

all sorts of interesting possibilities.

DAY 47: DOUBLE STOPS

TODAY'S GOAL

Most aspects of drumming require the ability to play several different patterns simultaneously. In today's lesson, however, we'll be taking a look at one aspect of drumming where the hands – although playing different parts of the kit – play exactly the same thing.

EXERCISES

At some point – perhaps on beat 4 at the start of a tune – I'm sure you've played the floor tom and snare together to create a thick-sounding accent, or maybe you've hit the snare and cymbal together to punctuate a certain figure. In today's lesson, we're going to put your togetherness to the test and take this a step further by adding the bass drum to the equation and creating longer phrases. This idea of having both hands punctuating the same figure is often known as playing a *double stop*. These can be played all around the kit, often using the bass drum to fill in those notes not played with the hands.

QUOTE FOR THE DAY

When I'm in practice mode, wow! The idea of being able to possibly play an intended new drum move over and over makes me really happy. I just do buckets of repetitions after I learn the basic move. – *Mike Manglni*

Example 1 shows a variety of combinations of eighth notes between the snare drum and bass drum. However, although only written on the snare, both the hands should play these parts, and here keeping the right hand on the floor tom and the left on the snare is a good place to start. Other possible orchestrations are:

Drums

- Right hand low tom/left hand high tom

- Right hand low tom/left hand hi-hat

- Right hand cymbal/left hand snare

- Right hand snare/left hand cymbal

- Right hand hi-hat/left hand snare

- Right hand snare/left hand hi-hat

Example 1

Example 2 shows how the same fill can be played between the floor tom and snare or cymbal and snare for a completely different sound.

Example 2

THOUGHT FOR THE DAY

These combinations can make great fill or solo ideas and can be played over several bars, or perhaps even moving between different variations and orchestrations.

Drums

DAY 48: SINGLE-HANDED 16th-NOTE GROOVES

Earlier in the book, we looked at playing hand-to-hand 16ths on the hi-hat. However, at slower tempos it's actually possible to play the same thing with just the right hand. In today's lesson we'll look at developing the basic feel as well as bass-drum and open-hi-hat variations.

QUOTE FOR THE DAY

To make smart musical decisions, you can't just think like a drummer; you have to step away from your instrument. Make believe you're the producer, and listen to what you play like you were listening to the radio. Just remember that it's not about you; it's about the song.

– Kenny Aronoff

EXERCISES

Playing the basic single-handed 16th note groove shown in Example 1 should be simple enough – after all, it's just like playing a half-time eighth-note feel, in terms of co-ordination. However, things start to get tricky when we want to play some more involved bass-drum patterns. This requires a new level of co-ordination to be developed, especially between the right hand and foot. Example 2 shows a selection of one-bar exercises that look at some different one-beat permutations played on every beat on the bass drum. Stay with each one until you feel all friction slipping away.

This is followed by Example 3, which shows some grooves designed to consolidate your new-found bass-drum independence.

 Example 1

 Example 2

 Example 3

Drums

It's also possible to incorporate open hi-hats by keeping the heel down and playing quarter notes with the left foot. This requires a certain degree of further co-ordination, but it's well worth effort. Example 4 shows a basic pattern, along with the last bar from Example 3 played this way.

 Example 4

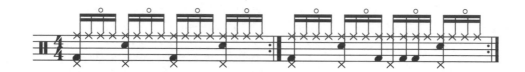

 THOUGHT FOR THE DAY

This is a challenging feel to play, especially when the tempo picks up. Legendary session drummer Jeff Porcaro used to be able to play this at incredible speed, often using it instead of hand-to-hand 16ths, which he said felt stiff by comparison.

For an extra challenge, try playing fills where the right hand – which has grown used to playing 16ths on the hi-hat – then has to switch back down to eighth notes to play a 16th-note fill down the toms. Try playing a fill every few measures to address this.

DAY 49

WEEK 7 TEST

This test track is written around a single-handed 16th-note idea and is based on a relaxed indie-rock feel.

QUOTE FOR THE DAY

There's an aspect of playing well that has to do with not caring too much. 'Detach yourself from the world' is a phrase that is prevalent in almost all religions. It applies to music, too. – *Billy Ward*

THE TRACK

Today's track begins with a two-bar drum intro that sets up the feel for the rest of the tune. The band enters at A, which is a 16-bar sequence. At B, it's up to the ride cymbal and a slight change in bass-drum pattern in order to move with the bass. These A/B sections then repeat, and the second time around the band drops out, leaving the piano playing. After three bars, the drums enter with a big fill and the time resumes for another eight bars. Here, it's back to the B section for eight bars and then into the final A section, which slows through the seventh bar to end on beat 1 of the eighth bar.

Drums

🕐 **10** **Week 7 test track**

Track 50 **Indie rock**

Drums

THOUGHT FOR THE DAY

This track relies on the consistent 16th-note feel generated by the right hand, so be sure to keep it as smooth as possible. If the bass-drum parts are proving difficult and affecting the flow of the hi-hat, try using a simplified bass-drum pattern.

WEEK 8

DAY 50: SIX-STROKE ROLLS

TODAY'S GOAL

Today's lesson looks at a very useful fill idea based around simple triplet-based sticking. This *six-stroke roll*, as it's often known, can be used in many different situations, from a simple Motown fill to a solo idea that can be moved around the kit.

EXERCISES

Example 1 shows four eighth-note-triplet-based accent patterns based around a simple sticking idea. In these exercises, if an accent is played on the first partial of

QUOTE FOR THE DAY

The three terrors of repetition, stagnation and utter humiliation usually help me stay focused. I only have to think of those three headless horsemen to get right up and start practising. – *Bill Bruford*

the triplet, a RLL sticking is used, and if an accent is played on the last partial of the triplet, a RRL sticking is used.

4X10 Example 1

Track 51

The sticking that appears in the last bar of Example 1 demonstrates the six-stroke roll. Example 2a shows it in its simplest form, played over two beats. Try moving the

Drums

accents off the snare drum and around the kit whilst keeping the unaccented beat on the snare.

Things begin to get interesting when we add three extra notes using the RLL sticking (Example 2b), taking the figure into 3/4. Joining two of these 3/4 figures and one of the original figures together creates a really interesting two-bar phrase (Example 2c).

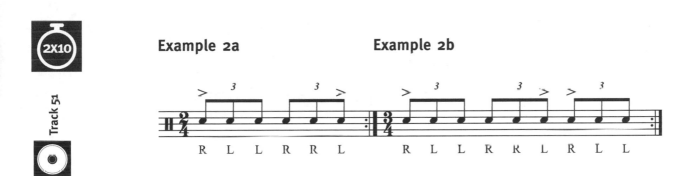

Example 2a   **Example 2b**

Example 2c

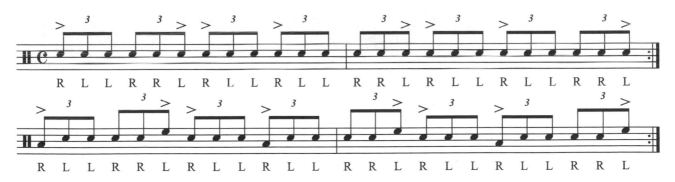

The basic six-stroke figure also applies well to 4/4, as a 16th-note-triplet fill, as shown in Example 3a, moving here off the first tom and onto the snare. In Example 3b, the right hand moves from the high tom to the low tom. This kind of fill can be heard on many Motown tracks, particularly in the way shown in Example 4.

Drums

Example 3a   **Example 3b**

R L L R R L R   R L L R R L R   R L L R R L R

Example 4

R L L R R L R

THOUGHT FOR THE DAY

You'll be surprised at just how much mileage can be had from this simple

sticking, so be sure to explore some different orchestrations. Try playing the

last left (RLLRRL) off the hi-hat, for example.

DAY 51: 6/6/4 COMBINATIONS

TODAY'S GOAL

Throughout the book we've looked at a variety of stickings, and today's lesson combines several to create a fun and challenging exercise.

QUOTE FOR THE DAY

Between constantly practising and being on tour and teaching a bunch of students, I'm always up on my instrument. I don't want anyone to ever see me play and think I sucked. – *Travis Barker*

EXERCISES

All of the examples in this lesson are based around the combination 6/6/4 – in other words, two groups of six and one of four adding up to create 16 notes. For ease of reading, the exercises shown here are written as eighth notes, although they can be played as 16th or 32nd notes, etc. In all of these exercises, the last four notes are always based around our single-paradiddle sticking – RLRR, LRLL (apart from Example 5, which uses an inverted sticking, but more of that in a minute) – while the groups of sixes move through a variety of stickings. You'll also find that each of the exercises switches hands when the 6/6/4 sequence repeats, which makes them great for developing technique as both hands are being worked on equally.

In Example 1, our groups of six are made up of double paradiddles. Example 2, meanwhile, uses exactly the same sticking, only this time with two accents added to each double paradiddle. Next up, Example 3 uses the paradiddle-diddle, with the sticking again switching hands on repeat. Example 4 uses a RLLRRL sticking in which the first right is accented and the second and third unaccented.

Drums

Finally, Example 5 uses the six-stroke roll sticking from yesterday's lesson. This is the only example in which the sticking of our half-paradiddle – which makes our group of four – changes, in this case to RLLR, LRRL, which tends to sit better with the six-stroke roll sticking.

Example 1

R L R L R R L R   L R L L R L R R   L R L R L L R L   R L R R L R L L

Example 2

R L R L R R L R   L R L L R L R R   L R L R L L R L   R L R R L R L L

Example 3

R L R R L L R L   R R L L R L R R   L R L L R R L R   L L R R L R L L

Example 4

R L L R R L R L   L R R L R L L R   L R R L L R L R   R L L R L R

Example 5

R L L R R L R L   L R R L R L L R   L R R L L R L R   R L L R L R R L

THOUGHT FOR THE DAY

These exercises are great for warm-ups. They also sound impressive if the accents are played on the toms and/or cymbals. However, as you begin to pick up speed, be sure that the difference in dynamics is maintained.

Drums

DAY 52: HALF-TIME SHUFFLE

TODAY'S GOAL

Today's lesson explores how a completely new feel can be created by moving the backbeat in a shuffle feel.

EXERCISES

In a basic shuffle feel, the backbeat is normally played on 2 and 4, as shown below in Example 1a. If, however, we played just one backbeat in the bar, on beat 3, we would create a half-time feel better known as a *half-time shuffle* (Example 1b).

QUOTE FOR THE DAY

Feel free to imitate the great performances of the past. When you do it, it'll be yours and will automatically come out your way. – *Billy Ward*

Example 1a   **Example 1b**

Example 2 shows some bass-drum variations to try. The first four are one-bar examples; the next three are played over two bars. As with our original shuffle feel, the accents on the quarter-notes in the right hand are important for creating the correct feel.

 Example 2

 THOUGHT FOR THE DAY

The half-time shuffle creates a wonderful rolling feel as long as the triplet subdivisions are played as evenly as possible. Two masters of the shuffle are Bernard Purdie, who played some great half-time shuffle grooves with Steely Dan, and Jeff Porcaro, who was responsible for the legendary groove on his band Toto's track 'Rosanna'.

Drums

DAY 53: JAZZ BASICS

Years ago, if you were a drummer, you were probably a jazz drummer – that was the only style of music being played in the early '50s. However, it wasn't long before rock 'n' roll appeared and music became much more diverse. These days, most drummers don't start off playing jazz any more, and unfortunately some don't even take the time to explore it at all! In today's lesson, we're going to delve into basic jazz time playing and have a look at how it differs from the drumming looked at so far.

QUOTE FOR THE DAY

When I started listening to jazz, I didn't understand the music, but I thought, 'These guys wouldn't have any problems playing *any* kind of music. I want to be able to do that.' – *John Otto*

EXERCISES

In pop and rock music, we rely on the bass drum and snare to define the time, and with nothing else playing listeners will tap their feet to just these two sounds, which we then tie together using either the hi-hat or ride cymbal. In jazz, however, things are different; the bass and snare still play a role, but the lead voice is the ride cymbal, followed by the hi-hat. In jazz, just these two sounds will get listeners tapping their feet, as this is where time is stated. The bass drum and snare are then incorporated to support the music, but at a much lower volume than they're used in a pop or rock setting.

Jazz time on the ride cymbal is based around an eighth-note-triplet feel, almost like the shuffle but with a couple of notes missing, as shown in Example 1a. This is accompanied by the hi-hat playing 2 and 4 (Example 1b), forming our basic feel. This is to jazz what our first eighth-note groove is to rock and pop. We can also use the bass drum to help pin this down by playing quarter notes, although these are nothing like our four-on-the-floor disco quarter notes, in so much as they need to be felt rather than heard. Playing the bass drum this way is called *feathering*, and it's much easier to do heel-down rather than heel-up, as shown in Example 1c.

Example 1a   **Example 1b**

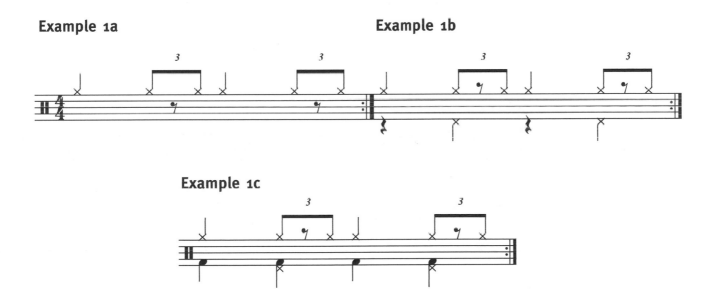

Example 1c

Next up is the left hand, which, instead of playing a backbeat, we can use to spice up the basic feel. However, in order to do this, we first need to develop some independence between the limbs. The remaining examples show some different left-hand figures played along with the rest of the parts. These can be really challenging at first, as the right hand will probably want to mimic the left and vice versa.

Drums

 Example 2

Track 54

 THOUGHT FOR THE DAY

Even if you've no intention of playing any jazz, the co-ordination that you develop here will really help all of your triplet-based playing. And, as I mentioned earlier, as music has diversified, other styles have been influenced by jazz, from blues to soul, hip-hop to funk. You need only take a look at tomorrow's lesson to see the connection.

DAY 54: HIP-HOP

TODAY'S GOAL

At first glance, it might be hard to see the connection between Eminem and John Coltrane, but the roots of the swung-hip-hop feel lie undeniably in jazz, and today's lesson explores this connection.

In yesterday's lesson, we looked at the basic jazz time pattern. Well, today we're going to step back and look at It from a different angle.

QUOTE FOR THE DAY

You're not up there playing to glorify yourself; it should be for a much larger reason. The music has been given to us, and you have to think of it as a gift.

– Brian Blade

EXERCISES

Let's begin with our basic jazz time feel, with the jazz ride pattern and playing 2 and 4 on the hi-hat, as shown in Example 1. Now let's add a bass-drum on beat 1 and a snare on beat 3 (Example 1b). This gives us a basic hip-hop feel, only, instead of it being counted as '1, 2, 3, 4', it's felt as a two-bar phrase with the first bass drum being 1, the first snare 2, the second bass drum 3 and the second snare 4 (Example 2).

Example 1a   **Example 1b**

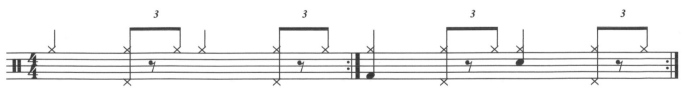

Drums

Example 2

This kind of feel is very similar to the half-time shuffle feel looked at earlier. Both patterns could, in fact, be used in the same situation, with the hip-hop feel lending itself to quicker tempos because of the fact that it contains fewer notes in the right hand than the shuffle feel.

Now let's look at some funky bass-drum variations. (If you're struggling with maintaining the jazz ride pattern, you might find it easier to look back at yesterday's lesson and spend a little more time getting the right hand to the point where it begins to play itself.) Example 3 shows some different bass-drum patterns. All of these exercises can be played with the right hand on the hi-hat, too.

Example 3

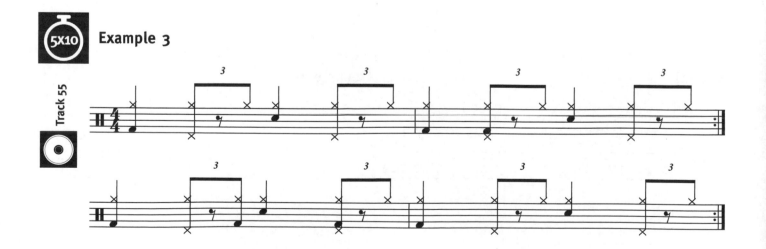

Drums

Example 3 continued

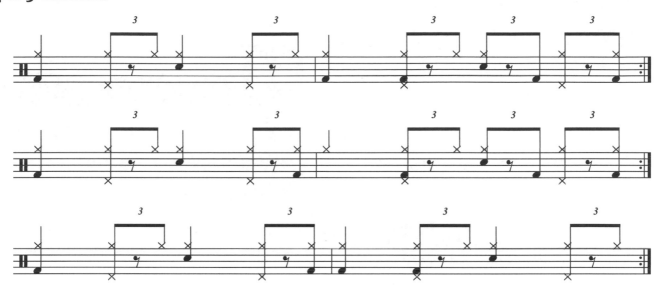

 THOUGHT FOR THE DAY

This is a tricky feel to play, but it's even more difficult without an understanding of the jazz time feel. At quicker tempos, you could remove the skip note from the right-hand part and play just quarter notes (which actually feel more like eighth notes) whilst still swinging all of the upbeat swung eighths.

DAY 55: REGGAE

TODAY'S GOAL

After the swung direction of the last few days' lessons, we couldn't really leave things without a brief excursion into the world of reggae drumming, could we? Today we'll take a look at the essential feels.

QUOTE FOR THE DAY

The hardest thing to do in any creative endeavour is to get started. The second hardest thing is to keep going.

– *Bill Bruford*

EXERCISES

Probably the most frequently used reggae feel is what's often referred to as the *one-drop* feel, named after the fact that there's only one bass drum played per bar. This bass-drum note falls on beat 3 and is often played along with a cross stick on the snare, after which we have a choice of what we can play along with that in the right hand. Example 1 shows three possibilities. In the first bar, the right hand plays quarter notes, accenting 2 and 4, which are also often accented by the guitar or keyboard part. The next bar shows the same feel but with a shuffle pattern in the right hand, and finally the third bar shows it played along with a jazz ride pattern.

Another feel sometimes encountered is when the bass drum falls on 2 and 4. Example 2 shows how this would look with the left hand continuing to play the cross-stick on beat 3, again moving through the three right-hand variations.

Finally, Example 3 shows another commonly used feel that involves playing the bass drum on all four quarter notes.

Drums

Example 1

Example 2

Example 3

When playing time, it can be nice to use the cross-stick for punctuation. Example 4 shows a four-bar pattern where the left hand plays a cross every one and a half quarter notes.

Example 4

THOUGHTS FOR THE DAY

Like jazz, reggae is a feel that no longer uses the same backbeat approach as used in regular pop and rock feels. As a result, it can feel a little odd at first, with all the space between the notes a little disconcerting.

One handy tip that may help you set up the atmosphere, when playing a reggae feel, is to tune up the first rack a quarter-turn on each lug. This turns the tom into quite a convincing timbale – a reggae essential. Another thing to try is to avoid hitting beat 1 after a fill; if you choose to, though, you could try playing the crash without a bass drum, or perhaps crash on beat 4 instead.

DAY 56

WEEK 8 TEST

Our final test piece incorporates several of the concepts looked at this week as it moves between a reggae and a half-time shuffle feel.

THE TRACK

Today's tune starts in a swung-reggae feel where, after eight bars, a back beat is added and the main groove begins. This section is 16 bars long, after which we move into the B section, the bass drum changing to a four-on-the-floor feel. After six bars, everyone pulls out at the beginning of the seventh measure and then re-enters with a triplet-based *tutti* figure. These A and B sections are then repeated, and after the *tutti* figure the second time around, the intro reggae feel is re-introduced. This eight-bar section ends on beat 1 of bar 8, where the guitar plays the lead into the solo.

C is also based around a half-time shuffle, but here the bass-drum pattern is different to that in the A section and is based around a two-bar pattern. This section ends on the last eighth-note triplet of the 15th bar, where the note is held for two more bars. Then it's the one-bar *tutti* figure, after which we see 'D.S. al coda'. (A *coda* is a type of repeat, and D.S. stands for *dal segno*, or 'to the sign'. In this case, the sign is on the top line at letter A.) We then follow the chart down until we see the target-shaped sign, where we break away and drop to the matching target sign at the bottom of the piece, where in this case the drums solo for two bars and end on the *tutti* figure.

Drums

Codas enable people writing charts to avoid rewriting large sections of music unnecessarily and direct the reader back to a previous section (unless it's marked 'D.C.', or *da capo*, which means you have to go back to the top of the tune). When you reach the target sign, jump to the coda and take it to the end of the piece.

 Week 8 test track

Half-time shuffle feel

Drums

Week 8 test track continued

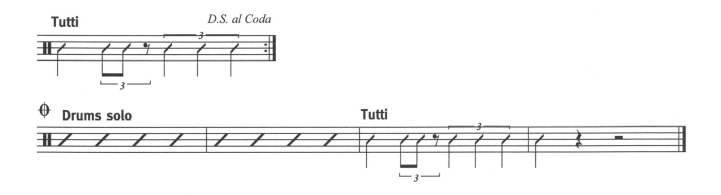

THOUGHT FOR THE DAY

This chart uses a couple of challenging feels that are difficult enough on their own, let alone when you have to navigate between them. The key really lies in the right hand, which, if able to maintain the shuffle feel, should help to hold everything together.

CONCLUSION

Well, you've reached the end. If you did it within the designated two-month deadline, you've probably just beaten any record that may have existed for the most drumming advancements in two months – and well done if you did! If, however, you just took it at your own pace, moving on only when ready, then well done again, as either way you've just worked through a huge amount of material which should have a massive impact on your drumming. You've developed reading skills, technique, fill vocabulary, groove ideas, rudiments and lots more, all of which you may not have been able to do before you bought this book. Give yourself a pat on the back. Now, what's next?

Well, if you haven't done so yet, I recommend that you get together with some other musicians and start playing some music. Find out how all of these ideas work in the real world, as opposed to the safe isolation of the practice room. Your nearest rehearsal room will probably have a notice board boasting a number of 'Drummer Required' adverts. Playing with other musicians is a completely different sensation to playing drums on your own, and the interaction and spontaneity involved is a wonderful thing to be part of.

You could also try taking your drumming further forward by finding a teacher. A good teacher will help you to keep heading in the right direction, as well as give you the help, advice and inspiration you need to become a better player. Or, if you're ready for another book to work from, why not try my book *100 Tips For Drums You Should Have Been Told*, also from SMT? This is a great book to look at as the next step.

Whatever your next move, good luck, enjoy your drumming, and keep moving forward.

Drums

ANY QUESTIONS?

If you have any queries regarding anything in the book, feel free to contact me via

my website at www.peteriley.net. Also check out this site to download bonus tracks

that missed the final cut of the CD!

NOTES

Drums